The Wray Flood of 1967

The Wray Flood of 1967

Memories of a Lune Valley Community

Emmeline Garnett

Centre for North-West Regional Studies
University of Lancaster
2002
Series Editor: Jean Turnbull

The Wray Flood of 1967: memories of a Lune Valley Community

This volume is the 47th in a series published by the
Centre for North-West Regional Studies at the University of Lancaster

Text copyright © Emmeline Garnett 2002

Designed, typeset, printed and bound by
JW Arrowsmith Ltd, Bristol

British Library Cataloguing-in-Publication Data
A CIP catalogue record for this book is available from the British Library

ISBN 1-86220-119-6

Contents

List of Illustrations

Figures

Maps

Acknowledgements

First and foremost, my thanks to the contributors listed at page [74]. So many people spent time digging into their memories, speaking into my tape recorder, getting out their scrapbooks, and answering questions. There were so many experiences, so powerfully recalled, all concentrated into such a short time, that it has not been an easy book to write. The height of the flood struck and passed in something like thirty minutes, so that trying to make a coherent narrative out of the patchwork of simultaneous experiences has been a formidable task. If the tale has lost anything in the telling, it is the fault of the compiler and not the contributors, and I can only hope that those most nearly concerned approve my attempt to get together into a coherent framework the event of that summer afternoon, and its repercussions.

Grateful thanks too to all those who lent precious photographs and newspaper cuttings for the illustrations, particularly to Robert Bassenden, who took most of the pictures of modern Wray, and to Jennifer Holt, who provided pictures of Roeburndale. The frontispiece and cover picture has been kindly supplied by Maggy Howarth.

EMMELINE GARNETT

The Millennium Mosaic, Wray, 2000 (By permission of Maggy Howarth)

CHAPTER ONE

Introduction

In 1998 Wray, like thousands of other villages, set up a committee to decide how it would like to mark the millennium. A spirited open-ended discussion followed, but with hindsight there was a kind of inevitability about the scheme which was finally adopted – the handsome cobblestone mosaic in the garden at Bridge End, completed in September 2000.

The inevitability was because Wray holds one important event in its folk memory – the flood of 1967. The ensuing years have seen a turnover of about four-fifths of the population, but no newcomer has ever been left uninstructed about the event of August 8 1967, when a flash flood of extraordinary speed and ferocity in the river Roeburn resulted in the loss of houses, bridges, livestock, vehicles, furniture and personal possessions. The stories of escape and rescue are dramatic, sometimes comic, and amazingly unmarred by any human casualty more severe than a cut thumb, and the result has been a body of shared experience which has played a significant part in building the community spirit of Wray. Community spirit is a difficult thing to pin down, but everyone agrees that Wray has it more than most villages, and that it has grown over the years in a spiral of cause and effect. Not many places with 500 inhabitants could have generated the Scarecrow Festival and Fair which in a warm May can bring somewhere in the region of 30,000 visitors; and not many could have supported the building, in the year 2001, of two extra classrooms on to a school with fewer than fifty children.

These two last events, the annual and the one-off, provided the original impetus for this book. The flood was clearly a fascinating story, worth rescuing from the past and preserving for the future. Starting very modestly with the idea of a pamphlet which might add something to the Wray School Extension Fund, the plan for the publication soon expanded. There were so many memories still vividly retained which would scatter and vanish if not collected in a durable form.

Collecting the stories has been a memorable experience. Some have been taped, some taken down in note form. (In the following pages speakers' actual words are printed in italic type.) What soon became apparent was that these memories were still extraordinarily vivid. Occasionally during an interview someone would dredge up a fact or an impression that they had not thought of for over 30 years, but not often.

Figure 1: Scarecrow Festival, Wray. By permission of Robert Bassenden

On the whole the stories were cast in the form they had first taken, almost a literary form, with few fumbles or hesitations. It is notable that some experiences had been taped very soon after the event, and were then retold for the purpose of this book with no reference to the earlier narrative, and there is no significant variation between the two. There are some people who, perhaps because of advancing years, have lost certain details, but the overwhelming impression has been that the memories were very clear, that they had been fixed in narrative form very soon after the event, and have remained in this form, typically a powerful and compelling one. It was very noticeable that when asked to go further, and provide information about what happened later, when the village was slowly returning to normal, people's memories blurred. Sentences became fragmented as they did their best to grope for details, and they often had to admit defeat. Some impressions of the first few days were still vivid, but the light faded quite quickly as the business of ordinary living took over.

Floods, like earthquakes and great fires, are among the most traumatic events to a human population, and in their extreme form, are things with which this country used hardly to be acquainted, though of late years our television screens have made us familiar with them in other places. We have seen the devastation of huge river inundations in Bangladesh, or mudslides in Central America, and recently, under the influence of warmer winters and deluges of unseasonable rain, various parts of the country have suffered quite severely from floods on many rivers. These have usually approached insidiously, with time to warn the population and fill the sandbags. Even if the sandbags have often proved to be not filled fast enough and not piled high enough, the resulting damage, though bad enough to the people who suffer it, is not classed as a national disaster.

All floods, in the end, are due to the same basic cause – too much rain falling on ground which cannot absorb it. But occasionally, owing to the lie of the land and certain other contributory causes, instead of a steady rise in the water level until a river, in the common and misleading phrase, 'bursts its banks' and spreads over surrounding countryside, the

Figure 2: Lynmouth, 1952. By kind permission of the *Daily Mirror*.

experience is of a headlong mounting rush of water from high ground to low, sweeping out everything in its path.

This is what happened at Wray in 1967. It was not a totally isolated incident. Flash floods of such ferocity happen more often than one might think. Indeed, the same flood on the same day sweeping down on the opposite side of Bowland Forest caused more damage, reckoned financially, in Rossendale than in the Lune Valley. The difference was in the human interest, because at Wray a village stood in the way.

Afterwards, the comparison that sprang to many people's minds was with the Lynmouth disaster of 1952. Another August storm, another network of small becks draining a moorland area, another fierce storm dropping vast quantities of rain on peaty ground already soaked and sponge-like, another descent of many hundreds of feet from the watershed to the sea, another series of catastrophic surges caused by holdups in the course of the river which then burst through with greater force. The differences however were great, and they were all in Wray's favour.

The West Lyn's fall from source to sea was not very different from the Roeburn's fall from source to the Lune valley, but on the West Lyn by far the greatest drop, some hundreds of feet, is achieved in the last half mile of its course, just as it runs straight down through the middle of the village. The West Lyn, and the East Lyn which joins it, end in the centre of a small gorge-like bay packed with the crowded housing of a bustling holiday resort. The Roeburn, on the other hand, emerges from the hill country to run round the edge of Wray village at the point where its course opens and flattens out. The Lynmouth flood followed a long steady downfall, culminating in a cloudburst of great intensity: it has been estimated that eleven inches of rain fell in 24 hours. The Wray flood was the result of a fierce but short-lived storm. The Lynmouth flood occurred in darkness, and continued unabated for most of the night. The Wray flood occurred at a fortunate time, in daylight, when the men of the village were just returning from work. It roared past, and subsided to a safe level, as quickly as it had risen.

In Lynmouth, 93 buildings and 28 bridges were destroyed at the time or demolished later. Wray lost a farm, thirteen houses and seven bridges. But the real difference was that in Lynmouth 34 people died: some of the bodies were swept out to sea or buried under the silt and never recovered. Personal damage in Wray, apart from the tears and the trauma, was limited to a few cuts and bruises. By quite extraordinary chance, everyone else walked off, stunned and shaken, but unhurt.

CHAPTER TWO

Roeburndale and Wray

The river Roeburn, tributary of a tributary which ultimately flows into the river Lune ten miles north of Lancaster, rises in the Salter and Mallowdale Fells, which reach at their height 500 metres above sea level. It gathers to itself a multitude of little run-off becks, many of which appear only in wet weather, during its five-mile descent to Wray village, which stands 450 metres below. It tumbles past the farms of Mallowdale, Haylot, High Salter, Middle Salter, Low Salter, passing under Mallowdale Bridge and the oddly named Drunken Bridge which gives access to Haylot and to Winder beyond. The ground is rough and steep, and none of the farms is built very near the river. High up, by Mallowdale and High Salter, there are virtually no trees, but lower down the banks are quite heavily tree-lined, remnants of woods once greatly used for the timber trades – house building, charcoal, tanning, clog-making – and left undisturbed wherever the valley's steep sides made it impractical to clear for farming purposes.

Barkin Bridge, at the bottom of a steep-sided gill, stands on a very old arch, the specifications for whose rebuilding in 1687 still exist.[1] It was awkwardly narrow for the increasing modern traffic to and from the Roeburndale farms, so, not long before our date, the parapets were removed and replaced by railings which splayed out from the road level, giving more room to loaded vehicles. Here the road and the river part company, the road climbing up over the shoulder of the fell and then down into Wray village, two and a half miles further on. The river continues through a steep wooded valley, twisting and turning through a chicane of rocky cliffs and outcrops, which broadens out about half way between Barkin Bridge and the village to allow of a small amount of farming land at Backsbottom. Below this again the sides of the gill close in, at one point into a narrow gorge. Here there is an old quarry, disused before the First World War, but which in the nineteenth century did a very prosperous trade in flags for roofing and flooring. In 1967 the track which served both Backsbottom Farm and the quarry crossed two more bridges and passed one more house, Roeburn Scar, a wooden bungalow magnificently perched above the river, before it joined the road that led to the village past the old mill. The mill itself was disused, and the machinery gone, but the weir was still intact, and there was a row of

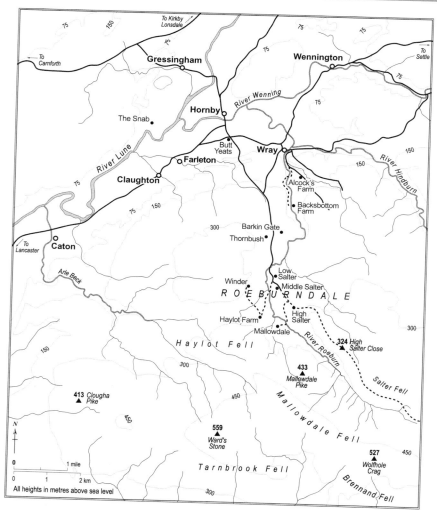

Map 1: Roeburndale and Wray. Map drawn by Chris Beacock, Lancaster University.

workmen's cottages along the road, and the old mill manager's house by the water side. Here was the footbridge called Kitten Bridge which in the past had given access from the village for people working at the mill. Some three hundred yards below was the last bridge before the Roeburn joined the Hindburn, Wray Bridge at the end of the village's main street.

Wray itself is not a settlement dating from time immemorial. It was deliberately and tidily established about the year 1200 by the Lord of Hornby Castle, who wanted to develop Hornby into a market town, an experiment which never really took off, although there are still indications in the present village of its enhanced status.

If Hornby was to be the town, with church, workshops, burgage plots, and weekly market, its inhabitants would not be available to till their own or the manorial land. This, it would seem, was the reason that a new

Figure 3a: The top end of Roeburndale above High Salter. The Roeburn itself is marked by the line of trees in the distance. By permission of Jennifer Holt.

Figure 3b: A quiet moorland stream: the Roeburn in normal flow. By permission of Jennifer Holt.

agricultural settlement came into being at Wray, which, tucked under the hill where the Roeburn joined the Hindburn, took its name from the old word for a 'corner'. As it was set up, a double row of homesteads faced each other across what became the village street, which turned a sharp corner as it approached the Roeburn, and continued downhill to a convenient crossing place at the bottom. In the early days the crossing was not a bridge but a ford, to which at some time were added 'hippings' or stepping stones. On the opposite side three tracks branched, as they still do – one along the Hindburn Valley towards Tatham, one straight ahead up a steep hill to 'Above Beck' and the Botton Fells, one turning back along the Roeburn Valley into Roeburndale East. The site was a good one, well watered and sheltered, on the opposite side of the large open fields from Hornby. Like all the Lune Valley villages, it was in the fertile bottom ground, but with the fell country for grazing close by.

It is still possible, with a fair degree of accuracy, to identify the positions of most of the twenty or so original dwellings in Wray. There were probably four or five between the turn in the road and the river crossing, and it is noticeable that they were built only on the north or high side of the track, well above the Roeburn: a feature of this river, as of so many in the area, is its tendency to produce sudden flash floods after heavy rain.

It was in the second half of the eighteenth century that the present solid and handsome bridge was built. This may be assumed from the fact that until about 1770 this end of the village was called 'Town End' and 'Hipping End', and then it became 'Bridge End'. It would seem that until the bridge was built there were no houses on the river side of the street, with the exception of the village smithy, which was high up, at the turn in the road, a good twenty feet above the river.

The eighteenth century saw a great change in Wray. For centuries, possibly since the settlement's foundation, there had been a mill on the Roeburn a little above the village, but that was the only industrial building until some time after 1720. Then, for whatever initial reason, workshops began to spring up, and an industrial population was attracted to the village, mainly nailmakers and hatters. They needed workshops, and they needed cottages to live in. They also needed water, and although the flow of the Roeburn is typically erratic, varying very quickly from

Figure 4: Wray Bridge End taken some years before the flood. The houses to the right of the two tall ones were all demolished. To the left is Smithy Brow, leading from the street to the river. Courtesy of David Kenyon.

awkwardly high to awkwardly low, it seems to have sufficed, if we draw conclusions from the considerable rise in population. At a later date the mill was greatly enlarged, and the waterflow problem addressed by the building of a weir and a mill leat. The problem was never properly solved however. According to a newspaper article in the later nineteenth century, the mill went bankrupt and changed owners seven times in the first half of the century.

Under the influence of industrialisation, the face of Wray had changed completely. Its old appearance can be seen in a village such as Arkholme, a single street of well-spaced yeoman houses. At Wray the spaces were rapidly filled in, a map of the 1770s already showing almost no gaps. One space which was developed was that on the south or river side of the street, between Smithy Brow at the corner and the river crossing, as shown in Figure 4.

Right on the bend, the walls of the village smithy can still be seen. Next to it is Smithy Brow, a space with no house on it, which has become a small carpark, with room for about three vehicles. Since the flood a wall has been built, but until 1967 this was a steep way down to the river, and at the bottom there was once another row of 'hippings', long since disappeared, but still shown on the 1891 Ordnance Survey map. The smith who was also a wheelwright used, it is said, to roll his hot wheels down here to cool in the water.

From this corner to the bridge a row of houses was built up at different times. It is difficult to say when or in what order, because some, notably the two top ones next to the smithy, have probably been rebuilt or replaced. All, except these two, were destroyed as a result of the flood. It is hard to tell from surviving photographs, but the three nearest to the bridge were believed to be older than the rest. In 1967 from the smithy to the bridge there were ten in all, with some gaps in the row. All of them faced the street, with their backs to the river, and small yards or gardens between them and the low walls which separated them from the water. Because of the lie of the land, the seven top ones had an extra storey, or basement, on the river side. The three old cottages at the bottom had none, but their back kitchens went down a step or two towards the river.

Looking down from the little car-park beside the old smithy now, one sees the river flowing placidly twenty feet below. In the memories of that traumatic day, this is the touchstone of astonishment and disbelief. Everyone with a tale to tell about the flood, regardless of their personal experience, wherever they stood and whatever they saw, inevitably says, somewhere in their story – 'And the water was coming over Smithy Brow!'

Note

1. Lancashire Record Office QSP 643/18

CHAPTER THREE

The Unexpected Storm

The Forest of Bowland area is no stranger to heavy rainstorms and sudden flash floods. The bridges have been built to accommodate them, and the farmsteads are on ground sufficiently high to be out of harm's way. That the flood of August 1967 was unusual if not unique is underlined by the fact that some at least of the seven destroyed bridges from Mallowdale to Meal Bank were built on very old arches, although the only one which can be dated precisely, Barkin Bridge, survived, but that was probably because, as has been said, its parapets had been replaced by rails. Meal Bank Bridge below the village, of which the piers at least almost certainly dated from the seventeenth century, was an awkward construction with a dogleg on both approaches, and a hump back like a canal bridge making it impossible for approaching vehicles to see each other. Backsbottom Farm, which was virtually demolished, was uncharacteristically close to the river, but its builders' confidence might be justified by their initials and the date of 1777 on a plaque above the front door, a date which marked the rebuild of an older homestead. 'Back Bottom' is mentioned in the parish register as early as 1668. The three cottages totally demolished in Wray are reckoned to have dated also from the eighteenth century.

It is in the nature of such fierce storms over the fells to be both unexpected and highly localised. The textbooks tell us that there are three main causes of rainfall in the British Isles: frontal systems, local atmospheric static instability (thunderstorms), and orthographic precipitation. This last means that in hot weather on high ground, warm air rising from the surface holds the disturbance in place above it. When all three combine, as they did on this occasion, the ensuing deluge may well result in what is commonly called a 'cloudburst'. On this occasion must be added the fact that previous wet weather had raised the water table to an unusually high degree. In other words, although at the time the surface did not show it, the underlying strata were as full of water as they would hold.

The month of May had been the wettest since 1729, all over the country but particularly in the north west. June had been fine to begin with but persistent heavy thunderstorms had been a feature of the second half of the month, and July was again wet and thundery with above

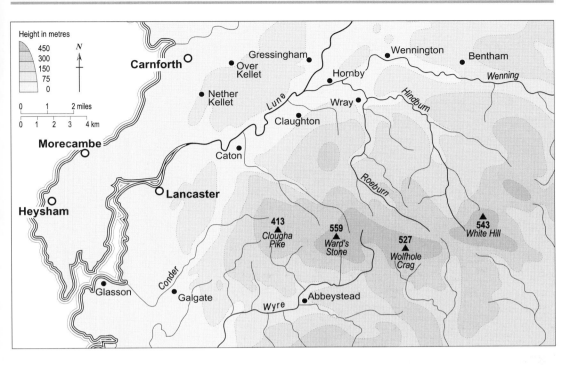

Map 2: Roeburndale and the Lune Valley. Map drawn by Chris Beacock, Lancaster University.

average rainfall in this particular area.[1] Patsy Everett, who lived at Roeburn Scar above Wray with the river running through the garden, remembers her husband commenting more than once in the previous days that he did not like its dark and peaty appearance. It was not at that time running high; indeed on August 7 it was certainly low. On that day Edgar Rawnsley, whose house was one of those built with its back to the river in Wray, looked out of his window and said to his wife that he was tired of seeing the tangle of weeds which had grown up on a little low pebble island in the middle of the beck where the ducks used to congregate He put on his gumboots, waded out, and pulled the plants up, throwing them into the small current.

Important though it was to those caught up in it, the event of August 8 was not, it would seem, of any great meteorological significance. No weather expert wrote it up afterwards. It is barely mentioned in the Royal Meteorological Society's *Weather Log*, their monthly summary of the British Isles. This does however give the broad background picture of what was happening to the country's weather in the first half of August:

> . . . *weather over most of the British Isles was cool with occasional thundery rain or showers and, as a depression moved across Scotland to the northern North Sea, continued so throughout the 3rd and 4th. . . . From the 5th to the 7th belts of frontal rain (associated with a deep depression moving south-eastwards towards south-west Ireland) crossed the British Isles from*

Figure 5a: Old Meal Bank Bridge. Courtesy of Robert Bassenden

Figure 5b: New Meal Bank Bridge: the old road is on the right. By permission of Robert Bassenden.

the west. . . . The depression remained off south-west Ireland on the 8th and 9th, but during the 10th and 11th the lowest pressure was transferred across England to the northern Sea. Violent thunderstorms associated with this disturbance caused extensive damage and flooding during these four, rather warm days, especially in Lancashire where at Hornby on the evening of the 8th, 77mm of rain [3 inches] fell in 115 min.[2]

(Hornby is presumably specified because the nearest raingauge was at Snab in Gressingham, about a mile from Hornby across the Lune. In the open valley, even such a weight of water was able to disperse with relatively little ill effect. Hornby's troubles were largely caused by Roeburn flood water coming down the Wenning.)

A later article from the Meteorological Office suggested an even more condensed and violent fall:

Thunderstorms, accompanied by heavy rain, were widespread on [August] 8th, 9th and 10th and were particularly severe in Lancashire. Falls exceeding 3 inches in 2 hours were numerous in the Forest of Bowland, and it is estimated that in the central Forest area 4.6 inches fell in 90 minutes. The village of Wray in the Lune Valley was devastated by floods and there was great havoc in the Downham-Burnley area. After a series of such storms on the 9th the flood damage in the Rossendale Valley was estimated at half a million pounds sterling.[3]

The estimated figure of 4.6 inches here quoted is higher than any other, but several experienced observers, including the Lancashire County Chief Engineer, agreed on three inches as a likely figure. His report drew on local knowledge and eyewitness reports:

During the morning of Tuesday, 8th August, 1967, although the weather was reasonably fine, fairly strong easterly winds developed, followed in the early afternoon by gathering stormclouds along the Western Pennine Hills; later a rather erratic pattern of heavy but short-lived rainfall was experienced in certain localities, although generally in the lowland plain between Lancaster and Preston. During this period of gathering stormclouds intermittent lightning occurred. Towards 4.0 pm (BST) stormclouds became intensified along the western slopes of the Pennines particularly at Caton Moor (height 1150 ft); the fells in the upper catchment of the Rivers Hindburn and Roeburn (height 1300 to 1400 ft); Dunsop Fell

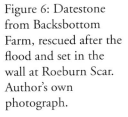

Figure 6: Datestone from Backsbottom Farm, rescued after the flood and set in the wall at Roeburn Scar. Author's own photograph.

in the upper River Hodder Catchment (height 1500 ft); and Pendle Hill east of Clitheroe (height 1500 ft). These peaks lie on a line extending some 22 miles in length in a south easterly direction, from Caton Moor (north-west extremity) to Pendle Hill (south-east extremity).

The torrential rainfall started about 4.30 pm at the north-west extremity involving Wray, and at about 7.0 pm at the south-east extremity involving Barrowford. The duration of the rainstorm appears to have been between 1¼ to 1¾ hours, during which time upwards of 3 inches of rainfall was generally experienced.

The intensity and violence of this rainstorm period obviously produced 'sheet' run-off conditions over the relatively small catchments involved and rapidly created chaotic flood conditions.[4]

The storm came in from the sea on a narrow path. Parts of Morecambe and Heysham suffered from 1¼ inches of rain falling in an hour and a half. The field station at Lancaster University recorded over 1½ inches in little more than an hour. But at Quernmore Park an eyewitness remembers no rain at all.

The weather forecast for the north west that day in all the newspapers was a variation of the *Daily Telegraph* 'Sunny intervals. Some light rain' or the *Express* 'Sunny intervals. Scattered showers'. It turned out however, to be a sultry hot and steamy day, and many people remember the build-up of a most unusually stormy sky. Tony Denby, who worked for the Council, was walling at Cowan Bridge.

It was a most peculiar sky all day, well, all afternoon, very close and hot, and it was black and yellow, we remarked a few times that day what a peculiar sky it was – yellow and red, you know a really angry sky.

Mary Bastow in Wray remembers a very strange, gun-metal sky, and rumbles of thunder all afternoon. Later, Edward Huddleston, living at Oakhead on the edge of Tatham and Bentham (it was his fourteenth birthday), watched the black clouds over Salter Fell, and the forked lightning striking down from sky to ground in the longest zig-zags he had ever seen.

When the storm struck, High Salter and Mallowdale farms were in its eye, but the Mickles from Mallowdale were at Kirkby Lonsdale Show, and Frank Ibbetson and his wife Margaret paid relatively little attention to what was going on outside. Margaret was busy with her eight-month-old niece whom she was looking after while the parents were away for the day. Frank had abandoned his bracken-mowing, because the sky was getting so portentously dark to the north west, over Morecambe, and had gone into the barn to clip a few stragglers from his flock which had missed the main clip. His old machine was very noisy, so when the storm

Figure 7: The crater
on Mallowdale Fell,
the moor untouched
on either side.
By permission of
Lancashire
Constabulary/
Gerry Forrest.

began he missed much of the noise outside, although there was one simultaneous flash and bang over his head which, as he says, nearly sent both him and the sheep into orbit together. Then he did look out, and saw the yard, which had been streaming with water before, at a depth of about six inches. The extreme downfall lasted, he thinks, about ten minutes, before it began to ease off.

The next day he walked the track of the storm at the head of Roeburndale, marked by the fiercely eroded surface of the fell. Up here the storm had stood still for a while, held in one place by the uplift of warm air from the hot moorland, long enough for the descending rain to gouge out a crater in the surface of the fell and, it was said, *roll it up like a carpet*. The astonishing thing was, as everyone who saw it remarked, that within a few yards of this evidence of savage power, the tussock and rushes were standing up unbent.

You could see the basic track of it come between Winder and Thornbush, up Haylot Bottom, and up between Mallowdale and Haylot. . . . Up Haylot Bottom, and back onto Mallowdale Fell, bottom of the Pike, High Salter, Low Close. It carried on, the track of the water, right up what we call the High Close, up on to Salter Bank, roughly following the old Salter Road, then it swung up on the top of Wolfa Crag, and them at Brennand and in Tarnbrook never saw a spit of rain. . . . it just dropped it on the top. I don't

Figure 8: The Fenwick Arms at Claughton. Firemen rescue a man from the flooded A683. By permission of *Lancaster Guardian/* Anne Jones.

know about Slaidburn, but I know Tarnbrook and the bottom end of Brennand Valley they missed it.

A line drawn on the map, following this description, shows a straight line, north-west to south-east. This was the eye of the storm but rain fell of course on each side of the line. Phenomenally heavy rain fell in Wray village, and elsewhere, for a relatively short time. People speak of raindrops bouncing from the ground higher than they had ever seen before, of wipers unable to clear windscreens, of being hardly able to walk for the weight of water in their clothes, of stepping out of a car and feeling as though a bucket had been emptied over their head, of finding their mackintosh pockets full of water, of looking, as it were, through a wall of grey glass. But up here was the central track of the storm which fell with even greater ferocity.

From the head of Roeburndale, heather, tussock, topsoil, peat, down to the bedrock, everything joined the headlong descent of water down the hill. Most of the damage at a lower level was attributable at least in part to the battering ram effect of fallen trees, but up here there were no trees. The power of the water alone and the tumbling debris it gathered in its path were strong enough to sweep away Mallowdale Bridge and the water supply pipe. Drunken Bridge below Haylot was the next to go. As Frank Ibbetson graphically describes it

> It's only afterwards you suddenly realise well, that wasn't there and that land, that hillside, were all trees, and now it's a dirty big hole, like. What were little bits of valleys, runoff places where you could stride over, you could bury a double-decker bus in. As time's gone on the sides have caved in and they've come back. You can't convince anybody what it was like, now. . . . Down at the chapel it had come down Low Salter yard, and lifted the tarmac up, one side were four foot higher, t'other side were a four foot pit.

As the torrent rose, undercutting its banks, it was augmented by fallen trees, 2000 of them by one estimate, hopelessly tangled and serving as a gigantic besom to sweep out still more of the valley bottom. And all the way the side-becks were adding to the tumult.

Wray was by no means the only place to suffer severe flooding, but the fall of water was highly selective. Caton village is built around four fast-flowing becks, which at one time drove seven mills, and these becks too are subject to sudden rises and falls. The headwaters of the Artle Beck adjoin the Roeburn catchment to the west, and if the storm had centred there, there might well have been far greater damage in a very much more heavily populated area. As it was, Caton suffered relatively little while at Claughton, the next village on the way to Hornby, the Claughton Beck flooded the main road (the A683) to a depth of three feet, swept away the retaining wall for 75 yards and caused considerable damage to property. Sooby Beck cascaded down into Farleton village, mainly striking Brades Farm. Police rescued the farmer from a small tree to which he was clinging, while his family took refuge in an upstairs room of the farmhouse.

The Kirkby Lonsdale Show took place that Tuesday, and accounted for a number of people not being at home. There was a short heavy fall of rain at the end of the afternoon, but the *Westmorland Gazette* was able to report

The rare event of a fine day in August's first disappointing week favoured Lunesdale Show when it opened the season of local exhibitions at Underley Park on Tuesday, and a big crowd in the afternoon brought smiles to the faces of officials anxious lest there should be a repetition of last year's deluge and financial loss.

(The *Westmorland Gazette* clearly believed in the sacredness of county boundaries. Neither in this edition nor any other did it mention any problems a few miles down the road in Lancashire.)

Notes

1. Royal Meteorological Society: *Weather Log* for May, June, July 1967
2. Royal Meteorological Society: *Weather Log* for August 1967
3. R.F. Booth 'Looking Back on 1967' in R.M.S. *Weather* April 1968
4. Lancashire River Authority: Chief Engineer's Report October 1967

CHAPTER FOUR

Backsbottom

Backsbottom Farm was the first habitation to be devastated. Built some ten or twelve feet above the Roeburn's normal flow, it was the only settlement above the village which lay directly in the river's path, and it caught the force of the flood. During the winter that followed, living in a caravan on the school field and waiting to be rehoused, Bill Brown wrote down the story of that afternoon. Not usually one to express himself in writing, under the influence of the remembered trauma he produced the following narrative.

This is a personal account of what happened at Backsbottom on the afternoon and evening of August 8 1967. This was the day we had fixed for our annual summer dipping of ewes and lambs. It was usual also to wean all our lambs at this gathering. Len Richardson, a neighbour from Stauvin Farm two miles higher up the dale, was coming to help us early in the afternoon. Sheep were gathered in the morning. Len was rather late arriving, having been delayed at home, and he brought with him a nephew called Harry Martin.

Dipping was finished about 4.30. It was obvious that a storm was brewing but the horizon was so limited at Backsbottom that we did not see the full extent. Leaving the sheep in the pens, ewes nearest the bridge and lambs near the house, we decided to have our tea before taking the ewes back to the fell. As we came round the barn end, a heifer which calved a day or two earlier came bawling to the yard gate. So I let her in and tied her in the shippon.

Richard came home from work just after five. It was just about then it started to rain heavily and I remember saying 'It's going to rain for at least half an hour'. Richard left to go to an evening job at Farleton petrol station, and now torrential rain was falling, and I was feeling rather frustrated and saying 'It's just like me to pick a day like this for dipping, it's all been a waste of time and dip'. I then looked out of the window and saw the river pouring over the garden. 'Hellfire' I said, 'look at that river, your begonias are ruined Alice, what a shame.'

Figure 9a: Barkin Bridge: the seventeenth century arch withstood the flood. By permission of Jennifer Holt.

Figure 9b: Below Barkin Bridge the Roeburn flows into a series of narrow gorges. By permission of Jennifer Holt.

'We'd better get those sheep out of the pens,' said Len. He went out the back door, I went through what we called the side door. Len opened the pen gate by the bridge and the ewes went through. By this time part of the pen wall had collapsed and water was pouring through, causing a strong current which the lambs could not face, they were washed back as I was trying to push them out. We managed to get a few out passing them singly to Len who took them to the higher gate.

Then Len suddenly said 'Get out Bill'. I tried to open the gate into the garden but couldn't, owing to pressure of water, then about two foot deep, so

Figure 10: Alice Brown's sketch of Backsbottom Farm. By permission of Alice Brown.

climbed the wall, and just got up the steps to the side door when the pen walls went completely, washing lambs away rolling over and over, rather a sickening sight. Water then was rising very fast.

I went into the house to see where Alice was. She shouted from upstairs. The water level followed upstairs for quite a few steps. I looked out of the window half way up the stairs and saw the bridge go just as if a bomb was under it. Alice was in the end bedroom and we decided that was the best place to see it out. It was then impossible to get away.

Going to the window I saw a cow being washed through the yard and across the little meadow under the wall which had not yet fallen, it found quieter water and swam out to higher ground. The van was the next thing I noticed, the doors burst open, the morning milk kits shot out, then the van itself made a right angle reverse turn and went with the current. I also saw the trailer being swept down. Before the buildings started to go we could see our family of cats darting backwards and fowards on the implement shed roof, then a crack and the whole shed vanished.

The flood by then was just about at its height, the noise was a great roaring, big trees fully grown were being swept past, downstairs windows were being smashed, the house seemed to shake every second as it was struck by trees and

Figure 11: After the flood: Backsbottom Farm. By permission of Robert Bassenden.

rocks. Up to this time although Alice was very frightened I felt the house would stand up to the battering and remember trying to reassure her. The next thing was a loud crunching crack and a cloud of dust. A small bat appeared in the room and quite a lot more light under the door, and we realised the barn had gone. I now realised the house could not stand much more, and we were in the hand of providence. We clung to each other deciding if we were going, we would go together.

After a short time we could sense that the crashing against the house was not so fierce, I looked across the little meadow, to where a haymaking machine called an acrobat had been washed up into the fence, I could just see the tips of the tines out of the water. After watching a minute or so I could see the water had stopped rising, in another few minutes I imagined I could see rather more of the machine. Slowly at first I knew the water level was dropping as more of the acrobat came into view. As confidence of survival increased I began to think and wonder what had happened to Len Richardson and Harry Martin.

Figure 12: Bill and Alice Brown at Backsbottom. By permission of Alice Brown.

Alice wanted to open the door to look out but I would not let her do so, I felt there was nothing much left of the house and for the time being it would be better not to see it. It was now only a matter of waiting till the water dropped enough for us to get out.

The next event I remember was seeing three youths coming through the wood across the other side of the meadow and shouting to us that help was on the way. Shortly after that our younger son Richard came running down the other side of the valley, with his hair standing straight up, looking terribly frightened. Although the water was still very noisy we managed to make him hear that help was coming and there was nothing he could do from that side. All this time I was worried about Len and Harry, I had seen nothing of them since leaving the sheep pens.

Men from Bentham Fire Brigade then arrived and after several attempts to cross a deep strong channel in front of the house, finally got to us via a ridge from further down the meadow. We were helped down from the landing about three yards from the bedroom door, the stairs having gone. The time was then about 8.30 or 8.45. Mr. Everett, one of his sons and Ernest Wright of Alcocks Farm were amongst the rescue party.

Figure 13: Alice Brown, 2001. By permission of Robert Bassenden.

We made our way to Alcocks and after telling Ernest about Len and Harry he offered to take me to Stauvins to see if we could find out what had happened. I still had doubts that Len and Harry might not have got out. I asked Ernest if he would go without me, as just at the time I felt I could not face Joyce, Len's wife, if Len had not got away safely. Looking back on this I feel it was cowardly of me. However in about ten to fifteen minutes Ernest arrived back with Len in his car. I cannot describe the relief I felt. It would have been terrible to live with the knowledge that I had been saved and Len had gone, through helping me. After leaving the sheep pens Len just got over the bridge before it went. He and Harry got to Wray by taking higher ground and arrived to see the bottom end of the village being pounded by water, trees and debris.

Alice's father who was living with us had been at Caton for the day and had managed to arrive at Alcocks farm, and was there when we arrived, he stayed there and Alice and I stayed overnight at Stauvins.

Next morning we started to sort things out and assess the damage. Any milk cows on the east side were taken to Alcocks to be milked, the ones on the other side were taken to Back Farm, they had not been milked for thirty six hours.

Very little was left at Backsbottom. The barn, and all the hay, shippons, loose boxes, stable, implement shed, pig sty, sheep pen and dipper, one end of the house which comprised of one room up and down, half of the second room, also upstairs and down, all downstairs furniture, all farm machinery and equipment had gone. Livestock losses were one pig, the newly calved heifer I had tied up just before the rain, one calf, some two dozen hens and between 45 and 50 lambs and one of our two sheepdogs, the other somehow escaped and turned up at Outhwaite Farm.

CHAPTER FIVE

Above the Village

The onward course of the Roeburn was not just a matter of relentlessly rising water. As is apparent in Bill Brown's story, the river came down in surges, caused by temporary dams building up and breaking.

Two surges hit Backsbottom. In a phrase which he used on a tape made shortly after the event, that he did not afterwards include in his written account, Bill Brown said graphically,

Looking out the window, I saw the river just boil over the garden wall like milk boiling up in a pan.

Then, while they were trying to save the lambs, Len saw a second surge approaching and shouted to Bill to get out. Bill, as he writes, climbed the wall, leaving the lambs to their fate, ran up the house stairs with the water literally at his heels, and from the half-way window

saw the bridge go just as if a bomb was under it.

With this surge came the trees.

The flood by then was just about at its height, the noise was a great roaring, big trees fully grown were being swept past, downstairs windows were being smashed, the house seemed to shake every second as it was struck by trees and rocks.

In the mile and a half between Barkin Bridge and Backsbottom there are plenty of narrow and steep corners which might have dammed. One can easily imagine trees, even a single tree, wedging in one of these clefts and rapidly building, holding up a huge weight of water and debris which then burst out. The ferocity of the main attack on Backsbottom and the rapidity with which it passed make one assume blockages very close above the farm, probably no more than a few hundred yards away.

It would seem that at least two surges hit the village. When anyone had time to gather their thoughts after the event, it became apparent that there had been a timelag between the disaster at Backsbottom Farm and the height of the flood in Wray. Len Richardson escaped across the bridge, scrambled up the west side of the valley, and, almost incoherent, battered on the back door of the Kenyons' house on the Roeburndale road, a third of a mile away. Once it was clear what he was saying, Richard Kenyon got out the van and drove him down into Wray, where he ran into the Post Office with the aim of phoning for help. Whether this was the call which alerted the Bentham Fire Brigade, or whether the lines were already down, is not known. Some little while later, Len found Gerry Forrest, and if the policeman's memories are precise, the flood was then just on the turn

> *Just after I got Dick Woodhouse out of the house, there was a fellow came down, Len Richardson, and he said 'You've got to help Bill Brown'. I said, 'What's up with Bill?' He said, 'He's in a terrible way' He said 'I was up helping him dose sheep.' He said 'I ran towards the hill, Bill ran back home to be with his wife' he said, 'and when I looked back' he said, 'the farm was surrounded by water, and the water was knocking the buildings down.'* (In another part of his story, Gerry says *I get him* [Dick Woodhouse] *out, and I'm going back up the street, and by the time I get to the top of the street, that river has gone down dramatically.*

Below Backsbottom lies the old quarry. Here the Roeburn flows through a narrow gorge, estimated at no more than four or five metres at its narrowest, and here the mass of water and debris must have piled and choked and then broken through. When Richard Kenyon went down to the Smithy Brow corner after dropping Len at the Post Office, a great rolling wave of water was lapping at the top of Smithy Brow. The universal amazement that water came over Smithy Brow is therefore a

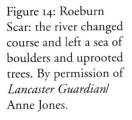

Figure 14: Roeburn Scar: the river changed course and left a sea of boulders and uprooted trees. By permission of *Lancaster Guardian/* Anne Jones.

little misleading: it was not a fair measure of the height which the river could be said to have reached. Because of the curve of the Roeburn, all the power was on the village side, the crest of the water, Richard thought, at least ten foot higher than on the opposite side, where the flood was spreading out comparatively calmly, over the road, the Holme Meadow, and up to the first floor of a row of three cottages.

The force that swept down from the old quarry is sharply underlined by a later observation made by Gerry Forrest.

> The road to Bill Brown's farm went through the quarry, and on either side there was a massive stone where they'd had to cut through to make a road through. And it was a massive stone, it must have been all of, oh, about ten foot high and it must have been ten foot by about six foot by six foot – a massive stone they'd cut through. After the flood, that stone was about six hundred yards down the river. So that's an indication – it had been uprooted and rolled down.

Between the quarry and the village, on a high bluff overlooking the river, stood the timber bungalow belonging to Mr and Mrs Everett. He was recently retired, and a more than enthusiastic gardener. The spot they had chosen to build was ideal. The Roeburn looped round below the house, contained by natural wooded cliffs, and the garden was contained in the loop, reached by a bridge which also carried the track going upstream, past the old quarry and up to Backsbottom Farm. On that day the Everetts had gone to Kirkby Lonsdale Show, taking the old car, not the new green Austin Westminster that Bobbie Everett had indulged in as a retirement present to himself. When they saw their property again that evening, the Roeburn had cut itself a new bed. The garden and the loop of river and the bridge had gone, and the river charged directly down a new straight channel of raw and tumbled rock. A piece of the verandah at the front of the house, high though it was, had fallen. The new car had vanished. It was seen spinning down the flood by Ivan Gledhill, a phlegmatic man who until that moment had been watching the rising water from his sitting-room window at the old mill house, sucking on his pipe and calming his wife: 'Oh no, he said, we've had spates before'.

The Austin Westminster, which he recognised, stirred him at last into realising that they should leave, but they almost did not make it. The windows burst and they were trapped by the rising water in their ground floor, unable to open any doors which would lead them to safety. Ivan got his feet entangled in linen from a submerged laundry basket, could not move, and Sybil was not strong enough to release him. In the nick of time they heard feet over their head, and a voice calling: a young neighbour had climbed a drainpipe and got in at the bathroom window.

The surge which almost fatally trapped the Gledhills was probably

Figure 15: Old Kitten Bridge. Courtesy of Robert Bassenden.

caused when the old weir above the mill went. Sybil Gledhill heard something cataclysmic while she and Ivan were trying to escape, but at what point is not clear. It was a tremendous access of sound to the roaring of the river and crashing of trees, so much so that in her confusion it flashed across her mind that they had been hit by an earthquake. What she heard was no doubt the fall of Kitten Bridge, only a few yards below their house.

The weir was an old construction, probably dating from the eighteenth century. Just twelve years before, in August 1955, there had been an emergency meeting called at the Lunesdale Rural District Council offices in Hornby to consider *the state of the stonework underneath the weir which was being washed away to such an extent that it was feared the weir might be in imminent danger of collapsing. The Consulting Engineer had*

Figure 16: New Kitten Bridge. By permission of Robert Bassenden.

reported that in his opinion the condition was such that a complete collapse might take place at any time of flood. . . . in fact at the time of inspection more water was flowing through and underneath the dam than on top of it.

Repairs were carried out a year later, by which time the original part of the weir was *in a very precarious position. . . . a further quantity of stone had been scoured out beneath the structure, and at one point there was little more than 18″ thickness left to the face of the weir.*

However, the Chief Engineer of the Lancashire River Board was able to report that remedial measures *had had the effect of providing a much improved finished product capable of serving for many years.*[1]

Not, as it turned out, in the conditions which prevailed on August 8. Edward ('Archie') Meadowcroft saw the wreckage next day.

The weir: well, the weir was a place when we were youngsters we used to play round there, and we used to get the mill race going, and the sluice gate was in and everything, it was complete. But the thing had just been torn out, all the woodwork had been torn out, there was still some of the steel, some of the iron strapping, attached to the rock bed, but all the woodwork and all the stone held behind the weir was gone, and now the old millrace was probably fifteen feet above the base of the river level. . . And of course Kitten Bridge, which was a most beautiful little single-arched bridge with a pedestrian arch which joined the two parts of the garden belonging to Gledhills, was totally ripped out – it was such a shame, it was a beautiful little bridge.

Figure 17: The old mill manager's house (Gledhills'), is built close above the Roeburn.
By permission of Robert Bassenden.

Notes

1. Lancashire Record Office, RDLu, Minutes of the Lunesdale Rural District Council August 1955, September/October 1956

CHAPTER SIX

The Flood hits Wray

In the village, the storm broke before the river started to rise. Everyone was driven indoors by the downpour, and the bombardment of thunder at first disguised the sound of the river. To begin with there was some astonishment, but no worry. Everyone had seen flash floods before.

The thunderstorm broke shortly after five o'clock. Tony Denby, dropped off at the bottom of the village by the Council van, walked home to Lower Broadwood.

I walked over the bridge at Wray at half-past four, and it was just a trickle, it was nothing, you know, just a little trickle of water. Got home, and Mavis said something about tea, and I said 'No'. I had about eight or ten cows, and we sucked some calves on them, and I said 'I'm going to get them in, it looks like a storm'. And I got them in, and it did come on a hell of a storm, and I didn't even let the cows out, I left them tied up, and came in and had my tea.

Ann Beckwith lived in the last cottage by the bridge on the river side of the road.

We had lunch, I don't remember having tea, but I do remember an emerald green feel about the whole atmosphere outside, and I thought 'Oh, we're in for some thunder. I'll read.' That's what I did, I read to Martin. The dog, in retrospect, was trying to tell us something, all the time, going to the back door, and then nudging me, and to the back door again, and coming forward and nudging me, and then the rain started.

June Swindlehurst, at the top of the same row, was in the street-level living room with her two children.

I was in the house, I'd been in the house all afternoon, it was a very very hot humid day, extremely hot indeed, and towards teatime...I guess about fiveish, again I'm not clear about that but probably about fiveish, it had been very hot and humid, we were in the house and I'd been cooking tea, we were having sausages, I remember it clearly, they were under the grill, and the clouds started to gather in the sky, it became very dark, very dark, black, and then it started to rain, and then the thunder and lightning

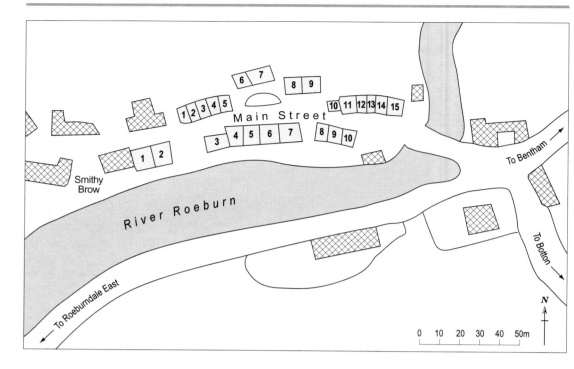

Main Street
Smithy
Brow
River Roeburn
To Roeburndale East
To Bentham
To Bolton
N
0 10 20 30 40 50m

started, and it was a violent storm. The children were both frightened, I think Susan was about ten and Nick about seven, and so we sat in the sitting room, and I said 'Come and sit next to me and we'll read a story until this is finished'. They sat on either side of me, I was reading a story, and the lightning was so violent I drew the curtains to shut it out, because I didn't like it very much either.

Map 3: Houses affected by the flood. Numbers refer to Appendix 1. Redrawn by Chris Beacock, Lancaster University.

Behind drawn curtains, trying to keep their attention on the story, they had no idea that the thunderstorm had in fact given way to the noise of the rising flood.

It seemed to get worse and worse, and the thunder was right overhead, shaking the house it seemed, and I heard a very strange sort of banging, rattling noise in the cellar, and I thought 'The wind has got up, I've left the basement door open and the doors are banging.' And I said to the children 'I'll just go down and close those doors', so I went to the top of the basement steps...stood at the top of the steps at ground level, at street level, opened the cellar door and looked down the steps, and all I could see was brown water at the bottom of the steps... I looked out of the landing window, and all I could see outside was a lake of brown, rushing water, with a noise like a train, a thundering train. And I looked out, and I thought 'My godfathers, I don't know what's going on, but we've got to get out of this'. So I went back to the children and I took each of them by the hand, and we went out of the front door. . . .

Next-door to the Swindlehursts, Anne Carrington was not at work because her grandmother had hurt her leg and in a calliper could not be left alone. Her father came back from work. There was a strange noise – 'You've left the kettle on,' he said, but it was not the kettle and it rapidly rose to a roar. She looked out of the window and saw an approaching rolling wave '*like the Severn Bore*', and ducks scuttling and scrabbling desperately in front of it. She went downstairs to the garden, to see the water rising inexorably up the garden wall, and then over it. Frightened, she ran back in, and locked the door behind her. Then she went down the row to the Denbys' where the water was beginning to come through the fireplace. She helped them move some things out of the way before, thinking of her grandmother, she ran back home.

All down the line of cottages, a similar experience was repeated as the water rose over the wall, over the little gardens, and began to seep into the back doors of the houses. Alice Wright rang her son Chris at Curwen Hill, a farm just outside Wray on the Lancaster road, to ask him to come round and turn the electricity off because the water was coming into her basement and her husband had not yet come back from work. He made a joke about bringing his fishing rod but all the same, having stopped silaging because of the rain, he got in his car and drove down to the village. When he got to his mother's house, the water was half-way up the basement stairs, and turning off the electricity was not an option. By the time they came out he only just got his car away up the little lane by Holme Farm, with the water up to the hubcaps.

Ann Beckwith says: *I went to the back door, and saw water (and this is a nightmare thing that I often get), it was a filthy coloured mud that was coming under the door.*

At that moment vehicles were still crossing the bridge, and a lorry-driver of her acquaintance, coming from Bentham, stopped at her door, and said 'I think you should get out.' She sent Martin across the road to Mrs Holmes, but stayed a bit longer herself, moving things out of the way of the water. Sheba the dog, taking advantage of the open door, ran for her life and was brought back from Roeburndale next day. As the water continued to rise, Ann went across to the neighbours to fetch Martin and go higher up.

When I stepped out of the front door, it was about calf high, and it had been dry when Martin went up. I forgot about the dog, my immediate thought was Martin. I went up to the Holmeses, and took him by the hand, and said to Mr and Mrs Holmes 'Are you going to be all right?' And Jack said 'We'll stay here. If it rises any further, we'll go down with the ship'.

Next door to the Holmes, Nicky Bogdanoff was watching from Helen Savage's house. The little French boy always spent his summer holidays with Helen, who had been his nanny. On this occasion his parents were there as well, come for a day or two to take him back to Paris with them. They had been into Lancaster to the model shop (Nicky always saved his pocket money for mechanical toys until he came to England), and had been glad to get back before the storm. They saw the water rising, but Helen said 'We're all right here'.

On the same side of the road as the Holmes, but nearer the bridge and therefore lower down, lived Ruth Whittam. Her husband Jack had gone down to Hornby after tea to fetch his car from the garage. These houses had very steep gardens behind, reached by steps which went up out of narrow yards outside their back doors. When the rain began to fall, Ruth's attention was drawn to the back long before anything disturbing took place at the front.

I looked through the window, out towards the back garden, and it was coming down the path pretty rapid. And as I was on a little higher ground than my neighbour, I saw it was going into their kitchen, and it was getting higher and higher. And so I put on my husband's mac and his sou'wester and some boots, and away I set out and ran around to next door and I said 'Do you need help because,' I said, 'your kitchen's getting flooded'. He said 'Yes, I know it's getting flooded but,' he said, 'three people can't work in this kitchen', he said, 'so,' he said, 'you go back into the house, we'll be quite all right'. I said 'I don't think you will,' so I went back into the house and I got a pole, a bamboo pole, it had been a curtain pole, and I went out at the back and I started to clear the grates. I started to clear his, and it wouldn't flush, and then I went lower down, and it did manage to go, and so the water subsided. And I came back, and I shouted through the window 'You're clear now' so he said 'Oh, that's fine', so then I went back into the house, took some of my things off, took my shoes and stockings off, and most of my wet clothes, and put some more on, and then sat down, got my sewing box, and was going to alter a dress.

John Wray was coming back from work. His was probably the last vehicle to cross the bridge from Bentham, perhaps the last from either direction. He got across by the kind of providential narrow squeak that turns up so many times in the story of Wray flood.

At the top of Millhouses Brow, I ran into heavy rain, and it was running down there almost like two streams on either side of the road. There was quite a flood on the road before we got to Wray, it was gushing out of the wood and filling the road. . . . When I eventually arrived on the bridge, there was an enormous river, swollen, I'd never seen it quite as

Figure 18: Roeburn View. The Carringtons' and Swindlehursts' houses. The basements were gutted by the flood. Courtesy of Anne Jones.

big. I actually got almost over the bridge, stopped my car, reversed back to the top of the bridge, and jumped out to have a look. . . . I looked downstream, and about twenty yards below the bridge there was a fountain almost, where obviously the water was crashing against something and spraying up a good ten feet into the air. . . . When I came along round the corner and up past the Post office, there were some of the Staveleys, Margaret in particular, hurriedly scooping up bales of hay or straw which had been washed out of the barn and filling the street. There was far more flooding at this end of the village at that time than there was down at the other end.

He said to his wife *'You've never seen the river like this. Come on, jump into the car, we'll go back and have a look'.*

They did, but in the few minutes it took to get back to the corner, having put on mackintoshes and parked the baby with his sister next door, *It was actually level with the top of Smithy Brow at that time. It was just trickling over Smithy Brow and running down the main street.*

Round the corner of Main Street, at Hoskins Farm, the water coming down the hill behind had almost filled the farm yard. The calves in the calf house were up to their bellies in water, and Bill Staveley was rescuing them. Water swept through the street-side barn, and out of the big doors, taking bales of straw which then broke up and blocked the gutters. Margaret Staveley went out to try to clear it away, as John Wray saw when he passed. She was joined by Gerry Forrest, the policeman.

That afternoon I was on duty down at Hornby, and it was a hot, sultry afternoon, so much so that we were in shirt-sleeve order. . . . We used to go down to Hornby to take messages at the station, we were always there if people wanted to produce documents or if they found anything, so it was mainly the collecting area for this area, the Lune Valley. And during that afternoon, about three o'clock, the thunder started rolling round the fells. As it increased in intensity, it still didn't rain, it got very very hot and humid, and at five o'clock I came home for my tea, and just after five o'clock, probably about quarter past, it started raining that hard that it was bouncing back up off the road, you know the type of thing. It continued to rain for about three quarters of an hour, you started to look outside, wondering if anything wrong is happening. And sure enough there was water being washed down the road. And eventually, coming down with the water, was straw which had been washed out of Staveley's barn in the middle of the village. When I saw this straw coming down, it was starting to block the gullies and the drains on the road side, and one on the carpark in front of the house. So I put my wellingtons on, and my waterproofs, and went out. And as I went out of the back door, there was a washing-up bowl which had been empty when I came in for my tea, and by now it had about two inches of water in this washing-up bowl, which indicated how much rain had fallen in such a short time.

While Gerry was assisting the straw-clearing, Thomas Huddleston, from Procters Farm, the other farm in the village, came by. He had just been over the Meal Bank Bridge on the Wennington Road to look at his cows and make sure they had moved to high ground. Some he could see, but some others were out of sight, and so high was the Roeburn under the Meal Bank Bridge that he did not want to be caught on the wrong side of it. So he decided to drive down to Hornby where he could climb the hill and look down on his cows in the Cow Pasture. On the way he spoke to the policeman as Gerry Forrest remembers.

I was raking this straw away from the drains, and the farmer came past. He said, 'You want nothing with that', he said, 'you want to get down the road,' he said, 'that bridge is in danger of going', meaning Meal Bank Bridge, which is on the way to Wennington.

Figure 19: Bridge End
after the flood: three
cottages and various
outhouses were swept
clean away. Courtesy
of Anne Jones.

The Staveleys' Landrover was at hand, so Margaret drove the policeman down to the Meal Bank Bridge.

And we went down to this bridge, which is a hump-backed bridge, and as I looked over this bridge, the water was about two foot off the bridge, but when I saw what was coming down the river, I was immediately concerned, because apart from car wheels and bits of furniture, the bit of furniture that concerned me was a white bathroom cabinet, which was quite new, not the sort of thing you would throw away. And I said 'Come on, let's get back, let's go down the other end of the village, someone's in trouble here'.

Margaret remembers that the bridge trembled under them, and that among the bits and pieces now carried past was a chair, a chair she recognized because only a few days before Mrs. Johnson had asked her in to the house to look at it. It had been newly refurbished, with rows of brass-headed nails, quite unmistakable.

We went back through the village (says Gerry Forrest) and when we got to the top, the bend at the top by Smithy Brow, we couldn't go any further, and there were a lot of villagers gathered on that corner, all looking down to the bridge at the bottom of the village. When I looked down, I couldn't believe my eyes, because the water was that deep it was actually lapping over Smithy Brow.

At the corner stood a shocked group of villagers. They had just seen the three bottom cottages vanish into the flood. Ann Beckwith saw her own house go:

The first real sign of how terrible it was going to be was when our front window cracked, and water poured through like tea pouring out of a spout, and the first floor windows were just cracked, and then it got higher than that, and water poured from Bertha Maughan's house, the three that were there, right through. . . . I turned to see the houses disappearing in a puff of plaster. And the whole terrace had collapsed.

Archie Meadowcroft saw it too.

We retreated to Smithy Brow, and from that vantage point we watched the whole proceedings. The river rose very very rapidly, visibly rising inch by inch, until it began to flow over the top of the bridge, round the bridge, and eventually the houses, the old houses to the south side of the main street, began to crumble and collapse. . . . One thing that did stick in my mind was that as these houses collapsed, only the roof and parts of the top floor were showing before they did collapse, but when they did collapse it was funny that in all that deluge and all that water, as the roofs collapsed there was a puff of dust. I'll never forget that. . . . And the sound was so loud that when the houses fell down it was like a silent film – the houses just, just disappeared, without a sound.

Nicky Bogdanoff remembers the same thing – that the cottages collapsed unrealistically, like models set up for a movie – like matchsticks. Against the roaring water they went soundlessly, which made the whole thing unreal.

Gerry Forrest found his own first reaction, as he took in the scene, quite bizarre.

I got round the corner, I looked down, and I could see that there was a gap at the bottom where there were three houses had been, and they were no longer there. And the water – it was – it was a raging flood, I mean that was the only way to describe it, and in this flood there were tree trunks coming down like juggernauts down the motorway, and they were causing a large amount of damage, hitting the buildings as they were going down. And I remember looking down, and I thought 'Where are the three families out of those ?'. . . . And I thought to myself 'How am I going to explain this to the coroner? because there's going to be no evidence whatsoever. Where are we going to find the bodies?' Because the river was so ferocious, I mean later on we had difficulty finding vehicles, let alone bodies.

CHAPTER SEVEN

Escapes and Rescues

It was a huge mass of trees, rocks, mud, broken buildings and bridges and a great weight of water, which had been temporarily arrested in the narrow gully at the old quarry, which rolled through the village. The arch of the village bridge did not give way, but the pile of debris which gathered there caused a tide to flow backwards round the bottom houses and back up the street. Other tides came through two gaps in the riverside row of houses and charged across the road and down the hill.

The noise was tremendous. Half a mile out of Wray, at Hillcrest, up the Roeburndale Road, as the worst of the rain slackened, Jim Kenyon got out of the house to feed his hens, and then went back in again to his wife. *'Something's wrong,'* he said, *'I can hear the river.'* Ann Beckwith is still convinced that as she escaped up the village she remembers a low-flying aircraft *'I felt I could almost touch it, it was so low'.*

The full force of the flood passed in a very short time, perhaps no more than half an hour. Time enough for some remarkable escapes. The riverside people walked (or ran, a neighbour irreverently remarked that the two Miss Wrays from Christie Cottage shot across the road *'like two startled old hens'*) out of their front doors. On the other side of the road, the Johnsons in the lowest house, the Bastows two above, and the Holmes, took refuge upstairs. Ruth Whittam, however, became trapped in her kitchen.

I thought 'Well, it's nothing for me to worry about, I'm all right here'. And then it started to come across the road, and it started to come in our gate and towards the door. I thought 'It's not coming in here' and so, we had a very strong front door that was new, and we had a vestibule door as well, so I thought 'Well, if I can manage to keep the water in the vestibule, I will do' so I ran upstairs and I got blankets, towels, everything I possibly could, and I opened the sliding door, and I got these blankets and towels and I got the sweeping brush and I pressed the door and pressed these things so the water wouldn't come in because I'd just put a new carpet down, you see, and I thought 'Well, it's not coming on to my carpet'. . . . And all of a sudden, as I turned round, the door crashed open, and the water came gushing in. And then the furniture started to come in, and I was trying to get through into the kitchen, and I grabbed hold of the grandfather clock,

Figure 20: Ruth
Whittam, 2001.
By permission of
Robert Bassenden.

*but I had to let go of that, because there was trees coming in, and
branches, and the furniture was collecting up, and so I ran into the
kitchen, and by the time I got into the kitchen, all the furniture out
of the kitchen was pressing up by the back door, so I couldn't – and
the water was, well, waist-high then, and so I jumped on to the
cooker, and then I went from the cooker to the washer, and then
from the washer I went on to the windowsill and all the plants had
gone off the windowsill by then, and I clambered on to the
windowsill and opened the little tiny window at the top and called
out, 'Is anyone there?' and I never heard anyone and so I thought
'Well, how can I smash this window?' I'd only little slippers on. But
anyway then all of a sudden the fridge broke loose, and it crashed
beside my legs so I thought 'Oh my golly, I'm trapped now' and I
tried to push it away, but the force of the water was bringing it
nearer to me, so – I had been cooking that night, and the pressure cooker
was on the top of the fridge, so I thought 'Oh my golly, it's floating on the
top of the water' so I tried with my hands to sort of make waves in the
water to bring it nearer, and finally I grabbed hold of the window with one
hand and I put my arm out and I managed to grab the pan, and I gently
brought it across the water and smashed it through the window, and then I
eased the other, the rest of the pane of glass, I eased it out with my hands,
and it sort of, with the weight of the water, it bundled me out of the
window, and on to the back flags there. And I forgot that we were sort of on
higher ground than my neighbours and we had to go down two steps. Well,
with the rushing of the water through the back I never saw these steps so it
bundled me down these two steps and I managed to grab hold of the little
wall, and as I grabbed hold of the little wall then I started to go up these
two steps and got on to the garden, you see. And when I got on to that
garden, I was just dazed, I didn't know anything, and these three men
came across the garden and they said 'Where's everybody?' and I said 'I don't
know', I said, 'I've just managed to get out myself,' I said, 'I don't know
where anybody is, and', I said, 'I don't know what's happening.'*

Donald Parker was one of the men who spoke to her. He had been
reading the newspaper at home, in the house just above Helen Savage's,
waiting for his wife and the children to return from Lancaster, where they
had gone to buy Sheila's new Grammar School uniform. The tumult
outside, and then a wagon driver shouting to him through the window,
made him aware of what was happening. His front door was clearly
impassible by that time, so he went to open the back door and was
knocked across the kitchen by the weight of water which had risen round
the house and now burst in. He struggled out and joined others who
went down the row, to rescue two old ladies trapped inside Bridge End
House. Miss Mashiter was aged 85, and her sister Mrs. Atkinson, 80.

When the men managed to push in through the half-blocked backdoor they found one of them clinging to the banisters half way up the stairs and one up to her waist in water in the kitchen. They got them out through the back door, just in time. It was Donald's memory that as they all clambered up the steep garden to safety, the water burst through the bedroom windows of the house they had just left.

When Gerry Forrest looked down on the raging sea of water where the terrace of three cottages had been, there was clearly nothing to be done on that side of the road. He started down the north side of the street, banging on doors and shouting to people to get out.

As I was going down, I was opposite Phillipsons', and to my amazement on the opposite side of the road, the front door was suddenly burst wide open, and a sideboard came whistling out into the street, and it indicated to me that the back of the house must have just got knocked off with the flood and the wave of water coming through had picked up this sideboard, smashed it clean through the front door, out into the street. And the thing is that you tend to disbelieve at the time. . . . The water was getting deeper and deeper, I had to make my way round the back of the property on the left-hand side, which I did do, and the first two people I came across were a couple called Holmes. They were trapped upstairs. I tried to get in to them from the back door, but all the furniture was jammed up against the back door. They were in no danger, so I shouted to them, 'Stay where you are, I'll go and get some help'. But in the mean time I made my way further down, and the further down I went, the worse the damage was.

The action was over much quicker than it takes to tell the stories. On the whole, people remember only fragmentary incidents, largely unaware of others round them. Almost in the time that Gerry stopped to call up to the Holmes in their back room, Helen Savage and her guests had scrambled hurriedly up their back garden, Ruth Whittam had been swept through her broken window and the old sisters had been rescued from their house.

The Bastows were helped, either then or a little later, from an upstairs window by another group of eager rescuers. They had taken refuge upstairs and old Mrs Bastow, aged 83, had climbed into a big cupboard in the front bedroom, as being the highest practicable level. From the window they saw the cottages go and with them two large petrol tanks from the sheds at the corner, which had just been filled with petrol. Mrs Bastow senior wrapped a large towel round her head, saying that if she was going to drown, it was not going to be with that smell. Mary suddenly thought of the new pair of glasses she had left on the coffee table in the front room. She went down for them, and as she reached the bottom of the stairs, there was a strange creaking noise, and the front

Figure 21: Houses on the riverside. From left to right, Wray's, Tovar's, Rawlinson's, Rawnsley's, Wright's. By permission *Lancaster Guardian/* Anne Jones.

wall fell in followed by a wave of water which soaked her as she scrambled for the stairs again, pulled up by her husband.

They broke the back window and people outside put up George Bastow's ladder (he was a painter and decorator), spanning the torrent which was running down the little yards at the back of the houses. Mary went backwards down it, guiding her mother-in-law's feet, rung by rung. Frank Costello was one of the rescuers and gallantly insisted on carrying Mary up the garden. He was only a small man, and they both fell into the water. Meanwhile Dora Robinson had found a wheelbarrow, and the elder Mrs Bastow was trundled away up the back lane to safety.

All this happened almost simultaneously. Gerry, making his way down the row, was able to say

And fortunately nobody else was in, except at the very bottom house. Mr and Mrs Johnson lived in the bottom house. I made my way to the bottom, to find out just what extent of damage there was, and as I got to the bottom, there was a fellow shouting out of the bathroom window, just a little tiny transom window, 'Will you help us – what can we do?', you see, and I said 'Get yourself out of there' because you could tell this house was in danger. So I said 'Smash the window – get out onto this leanto.' And I went back and asked for some volunteers to come down with me to try and force

*open this door where the Holmes were trapped, and also . . . there were four
or five people came down to help me.*

Word spread quickly that there was a dangerous situation in the
bottom house. It was one of the fortunate aspects of this unfortunate
situation that a good many men had got back from work and were on
hand. Gerry remembers John Wray, Terry Robinson, Bob Hebblethwaite.
John Wray noticed Dick Kenyon and Roy Dixon, and there were others
as well.

*Anyway, we concentrated on the four people in the bottom house, because it
turned out there were four people there, Johnson and his wife, and they'd
got visitors too. And they got out onto this leanto, which was sloping, and
the nearest place I could get to was another leanto which had a gap of
about ten or twelve feet between. And the water was roaring through this
gap in between. And to get them across this gap I thought well, the only
thing we can do is make a bit of a bridge. So I shouted to one of these lads
'See if you can find me a plank long enough to go across this gap'. So they
duly turned up with a plank, and you know it must have been miraculous
finding one just there and then, but they turned up with a plank, and I put
it across and bridged the gap between the two outbuildings, but through
leaning roofs it meant that the bridge itself was leaning, you know, it was*

Figure 22: The
Johnsons' house
showing lean-to and
outhouse, scene of
Gerry Forrest's rescue
of four people.
By permission of
Lancashire
Constabulary/
Gerry Forrest.

tilting. So it wasn't the most salubrious of escapes to be undertaken by somebody looking down because the water was tearing away underneath.

And whilst I was there, there must have been another blockage further up the river, because I remember glancing up and seeing slates coming over the top of Johnson's house, and this kind of galvanised you into a bit more action. Anyway I was a bit concerned about the safety of these people coming across, thinking one of them's going to slip, you know, four can't get across here safely. I said 'Give me a rope, or a clothes line' so, I think it was Hebblethwaite, grabbed this clothes line and threw it to me. I threw it across and the first lady, it wasn't Mrs Johnson, it was the visitor, a big stout lady, and she put it round her waist and I pulled her across, and by the time she got half way across I could get hold of her hand, you see. But she was that relieved she'd got across she just kept on walking and took the rope with her. So the next one across was Mrs. Johnson, and she was a little light lady, and I could get hold of her hand and she inched her way across. And don't forget this is a sloping wet board they're coming across, and looking down it must have been frightful. And then the fellow came across, the visitor, and when he came across he said 'Where's me car?' and I looked round, and his car was going, it was just ready for going. All he was concerned about was saving his car, and I don't think he ever did, I think it went before he got there. But then Mr Johnson came across, and he was shuffling rather unusually, and it was only when I got hold of his hand, he said 'I've got two false hips'. And I thought, 'What a marvellous fellow.'

John Wray, when he came to think about it, was equally astonished by what four people of awkward ages and sizes could do under the necessity of saving their lives.

I think Dick Kenyon and Roy Dixon turned up with a ladder. . . . I heard a shout from someone, and there was the first of the people across the plank, I don't know how on earth they got across that plank, I shall never know, but the first I realised of this was this woman being pushed along the ridge of this outbuilding and more or less into my arms by Bob Hebblethwaite. She was quite large, and how Gerry got her across I shall never know. . . . I didn't actually see anyone come across the plank, thank goodness, so I've really no idea how Gerry got them across, but get them across he did, and it was certainly a wonderful effort. The way these people went down the ladder, which was balanced precariously, was quite wonderful really. They had no hesitation whatever, they just went down this ladder from this roof as if it was the sort of thing they did every day. If they'd all been window cleaners I don't think they could have done any better really. And so they were rescued, they were safely out of the way and the house was still standing.

But it was only just standing. Gerry says:

When I was getting the Johnsons out, everything was dark behind them, and when I was getting the last one out, everything was light behind them, so the house was disintegrating.

And so back to the Holmes' house. Mr and Mrs Holmes had retired upstairs, reassured by the policeman, and had spent the intervening minutes methodically packing their suitcases. There was some three feet of water inside, and to get through the back door meant hacking a way through the wreckage that had piled up. It was accomplished, although Mr Holmes was very put out when, he and his suitcase both rescued, he found that it was still raining and he had left his macintosh behind.

Gerry's attention was called elsewhere. Directly in front of the Holmes' house, lower by several feet and abutting on to Miss Mashiter's much more solid building, was Dick Woodhouse's little white cottage.

Harry Robinson's wife, Dora, came to me and said 'We haven't seen Dick Woodhouse. He's bedfast.' And his house was directly in line with the flood. . . . I couldn't get in the front or back door because they were covered in –

Figure 23: The north side of the street: Dick Woodhouse, Mashiters', Whittams', Bastows', Hartleys'. By permission of Lancashire Constabulary/ Gerry Forrest.

the water was about ten foot, fourteen foot deep there, it was well over the doors, anyway. So I got up on the roof and I tried to smash my way through the roof, but there were these big stone flags and they just wouldn't move. So I went round the side of the house, and fortunately, debris had lodged up against the side of the house, the gable end, and it was pointing up to a little window, so I was able to climb up this debris and when I got up to the window I smashed it and shouted 'Are you there, Dick?' and he – I could hear this little voice inside, and I climbed through and everything is in turmoil. All the furniture is washed and tumbled about – nothing like a normal flood, you know, these are rough floods. So I went into the front bedroom, and it was a sight to see. Dick was lying in bed, the front window had gone, and part of the front wall had gone, and the water was just about level with his bed. And he was sat there, looking at me, and he said 'Now then', he said, and I said 'Come along, I've come to get you out'. So, as he stood up on the bed, I was going to give him a fireman's lift, he said 'Where's me trousers?' And there was a wicker chair floating round the bedroom – fortunately, his trousers were on that wicker chair, so I got the wicker chair, and he got one leg in his trousers, and he said 'Where's me underpants?' And I said 'Come on, we're not buggering about with underpants. Let's be getting out of here', because looking out of the front window, the level of the water, trees were going past like lorries, like big heavy lorries, and every now and again you'd hear a tump, one had just nudged the side of the house, you know, and I thought, you know, 'It's not the best place to be, in here', so him bothering about underpants it was a bit. . . . . So I got him out to the back bedroom window that I'd smashed open and I got outside and pulled him through, carried him down, and some villagers came down right away, because the water was beginning to recede, you see, it was quite quick, how quickly it did go down.

As Gerry modestly says, when he got Dick Woodhouse through the back window, *'a bit of a cheer went up'* from the people below. It was the last of the rescues and the water was already beginning to recede. Indeed it went down so quickly that he thought rather wryly *If I'd've waited another ten minutes I could've got out of the front door.* The village was battered, but its population safe. Amazingly, apart from Ruth Whittam, with a badly cut thumb from the broken glass of her kitchen window, one does not hear of any personal injuries. Perhaps the person who suffered most, though not physically, was Stan Beckwith, who relates his story with Anglo-Saxon understatement.

On that particular day of the flood I'd been working down in Yorkshire, and I'd been in and around the Hellifield and Gargrave areas, and I was making my way back, and I would assume that when the disaster struck, I was perhaps on the moor area in between Clapham and Bentham. And I recall how very dark it was over the Wray and district area, and I just thought to myself 'My goodness, someone's getting it round about Wray tonight', never dreaming of course what I would encounter.

And as I approached, I came in via the Punchbowl at Bentham, and I turned left, which would bring me to the village via Millhouses, and as I approached the bridge, or the two barns which were near Maud's properties, there was a tailback of cars that were parked, and I just wondered what was happening, because I had to park I think about four or five cars back and get out and walk towards the bridge. And I remember seeing Jimmy Swindlehurst there for one, I can't remember the rest of the people who were gathered around there.

One couldn't see the river from where I'd parked, because of the barns on the right side, and another barn on the left, which is now Mrs Staveley's property, and so I wasn't aware of the full force or impact until I actually got between these two buildings and saw that the river was actually flowing over the bridge. And according to Jim Swindlehurst I changed colour about four or five times. So – at that point there was so much water we lost all perspective of things*. I didn't realise that the cottage had gone at that stage. I was looking further up the village to the last remaining cottage, which I think was Chris Wright and Mrs Wright's, and I just assumed that that was ours.

There was so much water, it was so vast, I couldn't really gather things till I started looking at windows, and then I thought well, we didn't have a window there, and we didn't have a window here, and so on, and it was only then that it struck me that the whole small part of that terrace had been washed away, ours of course being the first, and then Bertha Maughan's and the Denbys'. It was quite obvious then that if anyone had stayed in the houses they would have perished. So the main worry was what had happened to Ann and Martin.

I decided to go to higher ground in an area which we used to call Maud's paddock, to make my way to Kitten Bridge, which was a footbridge further up the river, and I was just hoping for a miracle that that would still be standing and I could get into the village via the footbridge. However, that had gone as well. But it was in a way a blessing that I'd done this, because behind the properties near the Post Office and just further down Len Richardson was on this side, the other side, of the river, in other words I was trapped outside and Leonard who lived in one of the farms going up the back of the river, he was inside the village. And he shouted across, and he was waving his cap, and let me know then that Ann and Martin were safe. And from what I recall, I think he said 'They're all right, they're in the Institute'. . . . And of course I could relax somewhat then, knowing that Ann and Martin were safe. So I lost all sense of time, then, but obviously I had to wait on the other side until the waters subsided, and then I think I actually walked across, because the bridge was probably still covered with debris at that time, I maybe didn't get the vehicle across till the next day,

I'm not sure. And eventually I walked into the village, and well, as a family we were reunited.

*Jim said 'We looked and looked,' and Stan was saying 'Jimmy I can't see my house,' and Jim was saying 'It'll be all right Stan, it's just because there's water, it'll be there somewhere' but they couldn't make sense of the landscape, you know, and eventually of course they realised that Stan's house wasn't there, and he was so concerned, because his wife, and child – and the house had gone, just the foundations left, if that. Actually they had got – they had got out safely, which was a great blessing. June Drury (Swindlehurst)

CHAPTER EIGHT

The End of the Day

The catastrophic rise of the river was only equalled by the speed with which it subsided, still running very high but back in its own bed. The village looked round at itself. Wherever the water had been was a battlefield of rocks and debris. Three cottages, and a farm building just below the bridge, had vanished as though they had never been; seven houses backed on to the river presented a tolerable aspect at the front but were battered hollow at the back. On the opposite side of the road Miss Mashiter's house, though the oldest, was also the most solid, and stood firm. The four below, and Dick Woodhouse's cottage above, were smashed beyond repair. The arch of the bridge was intact, but the abutments had been damaged and the parapets ripped off. Water was still flowing under, but there was a huge trunk stuck in the arch, and trees and debris piled six or eight feet deep on the top. Two large petrol tanks and an unknown number of vehicles had gone. Elsewhere the main damage was from water and stinking mud, which had filled lower storeys more or less solid. (The smell was all-pervasive and something everyone remembers.) The twelve-inch sewer pipe had been severed and the new sewage farm below the Meal Bank Bridge was out of action. The water pipeline which crossed the Roeburn at Kitten Bridge had gone with the bridge. There was no electricity, sewerage, water supply or telephone.

Wray looked after its own, as Gerry Forrest remembers.

And they were all coming round, saying 'What do we do? What do we do?'
So I said, 'Well, get to the Institute, we'll have to organise something.
Anybody who's homeless, you'll have to go to the Institute, and we'll get
organised from there'. So they all pushed off, but by the time I got to the
Institute, all the homeless people had been rehoused by local people, which
was a good thing.

Everything had happened so fast that P.C. Forrest's superior, Sergeant Leslie Smith, the Hornby Sergeant who lived in Wray, and had been off duty at home, missed the height of the drama. Now the two men had the aftermath to deal with, and for a while it felt as though the world had left them in total isolation. In fact vague news of the disaster had got out; half a 999 call, probably sent by Brenda Stalker, had been received before the lines went dead, but broken bridges and blocked roads for a while prevented anyone getting in. In particular the A683 was flooded at Claughton, and there was a sea of water over the lower land between Claughton and Wray. To add to the difficulties, Claughton was well known as a dead spot for police car radios.

Archie Meadowcroft reckons that he was one of the last to get through at Claughton.

I worked at Lancaster University at the time. I left work 5 o'clock, and I was at the Fenwick Arms maybe 5.15, 5.20. At that time the small beck at Claughton was already rushing past the Fenwick Arms, and across the road, and some people were already hesitant to cross the water rushing across the road. I had an old car, an old Austin Ten at the time, which is a high-built vehicle, so I had no problem going through that water, so already round 5.30 there were problems. I drove on, and got as far as Butt Yeats, and continued towards Wray, to find that in the dip to the west side of Curwen Hill, the water was already too deep, there was a car sat there in the middle, so I turned round, went back, went up the Roeburndale road, turning back down into Wray at the first left-hand turn. . . . It was sheeting it down. . . . I know that when I came heading down towards Wray, towards Dick Hill, there were stones, large stones, rolling across the road, along with water from what was the culvert at the side of the road, and I had to stop, get out of the car, and actually move rocks off the road before I could proceed. I was out of the car maybe two minutes, just enough time to shift a few stones, and I was soaked. The water was coming down literally in sheets. The visibility was not good, and I'd never experienced anything like that in rainfall.

Figure 24: Stan Beckwith standing on the ruins of his house. By permission of *Lancaster Guardian.*

Half an hour later Pat Hayton was coming home from work in Lancaster on the bus to Hornby.

We got as far as Claughton, and we could see that the brickworks were flooded. . . . We had no idea what had happened, and it was quite a shock to find all this water. There was a fire engine in front of us, plus an ambulance, and we went very slowly through the water, following the fire engine, and there were some people in a Mini, I think there was two adults and two children, and we pulled them out of the water on to the bus, which was much higher. We went through the water, travelling very slowly, still expecting of course that we were going to get home to Hornby. We got within sight of the Fenwick Arms, and realised that things weren't as we expected. And all the traffic came to a standstill, so the bus driver got out to investigate, find out what had happened, and he came back with the story that the engine and the ambulances were trying to get through to Wray, because there'd been this tremendous flood. But still we didn't realise that we wouldn't be able to get home that night.

(There was at least one Wray resident on the same bus – Mrs Hartley, who lived next to the Johnsons and did not know that her house had been gutted.)

Hornby in its turn felt the effect of the Roeburndale water. A wall of water descended on the village and a number of houses were flooded, but the effects were less than they might have been. Where the Hindburn joins the Wenning, Junction Wood was in process of being felled, and a great number of the trees being swept down, which had acted like battering rams in Wray village, were caught up and lodged in the half-felled wood. Hornby escaped the worst of the battering that Wray had endured, and the bridge survived. Thomas Huddleston, when he had warned Gerry Forrest about the Meal Bank Bridge, had continued on his tractor to Hornby, intent on climbing the hill to see if his cattle were all right. As he went down, the Wenning was rising, but he crossed the bridge without difficulty. On the way back, water was over the top, and the Hornby fire engine was prevented from getting across. The tractor was sufficiently high off the ground to give the fire engine a tow through the flood to dry ground where it could start up its motor and go on its way to Wray.

Bentham, five miles away, received quite early information. It is not known how the Bentham Fire Brigade was alerted, but it seems to have been the first rescue vehicle on the scene, though of course on the wrong side of the river. James (Jimmy) Robinson was in charge and remembers that as they came from Bentham in answer to the call they wondered what was up. There were black clouds over the fell but at Wennington the sun was shining and there was nothing extraordinary about the Wenning River at that point. Until they came to Meal Bank Bridge and found it destroyed they were not convinced that it could be a genuine alarm. They turned back and went round by the Meal Bank lane and over the Hindburn Bridge half a mile out of Wray. Even there, in Jimmy's recollection, there was nothing extraordinary. It was not until they were stopped on the far side of Bridge End that they saw the extent of the damage. The river was still coming down like a fury, the bridge a pile of debris, and the water up to the first floor windows of the three cottages on the south side of the beck. (Mary Woodhouse, her two little children and her aunt had escaped through a back upstairs window and got to safety up the slope.) The firemen were able to conduct a shouted

Figure 25: P.C. Gerry
Forrest, 1967.
By permission of
*Lancaster Guardian/
Gerry Forrest.*

conversation with Gerry Forrest, and then, abandoning their vehicle, they took to the higher ground with their ropes and gear.

When I looked down, the Fire Brigade from Bentham were on the opposite side of the bridge by Margaret Staveley's, Bridge End there. 'Can we help? Can we do owt to help?' I said 'You can get up to Backsbottom and see if you can help Bill Brown.' Fortunately, you see, they were able to get up there, but all they could do when they got up there, was sit and wait for the water to go down. . . .

Soon after the Bentham fire engine, further useful help from the West Riding arrived in the shape of the Settle Cave Rescue team.

The Cave Rescue people appeared on the opposite side of the river. . . . at Bridge End, and they were shouting across 'We've got a land line, we've got a telephone land line, can we bring it across?' I said 'Ay, bring it across.' And they'd come from Settle, and they were used to doing this kind of thing – up on the fells they've got to get land lines to caves where probably somebody's life's in danger, you know, they've got to get a land line up, and they were quite used to it. And they had these reels of wire, and they came over this debris which was on top of the bridge. The bridge had been half destroyed but there was piles of trees just perched on top of it. . . . .They came across there, and up to the Institute, and got communication. . . . They were there within about an hour. . . .

We got back to Hornby to try to ring up from Hornby station, and whilst we were doing this, a police car made it through from Kirkby Lonsdale, and that was the first one in. Nobody seemed to know that we were in dire straits. . . . . Anyway, this police car came up, and when he heard my story, he said 'Get hold of the mike, and tell headquarters what you're telling me,' so I told them all, and they were then able to organise the people like the health people and the council people, and the fire brigade, and what have you.

It may have seemed a very long time, but by eight o'clock the gears were engaged and the machinery working. Tony Denby, after the worst of the storm, had gone up over his fields to see whether any sheep had been struck by lightning.

I met Frank Harrison on the top road, from Birks, and Frank just said 'Jump in'. 'Jump in', he said, 'I'm going to Wray,' he said, 'our Elsie's come back, I can't make much of her', he said. 'Well', he said, 'she's bawling her eyes out,' Frank said. 'And she said half of Wray's gone' — she was married and lived at Hornby, and she'd been up at home to see her dad, and gone back at half six, seven o'clock. So I got in with Frank and came down to Wray, and I couldn't believe it. . . .

I got co-opted for work right away, there was Council men there. . . . between eight and half past. . . . I was on duty, didn't come home while about three o'clock, at this end of the bridge with a policeman, stopping anyone coming into the village and until some council wagons — oh, we put barriers across the bridge down Wennington Road, Meal Bank Bridge. . . . there was a wagon came in there, brought some barriers, and we put that up, and then they came round over Meal Bank to this bridge [Hindburn Bridge] and put some barriers up there. . . . I was on with this policeman from Lancaster, and the Rawnsleys from Wray, they came back into Wray, just turned midnight, one o'clock. The policeman wouldn't let them come in, said no, they weren't allowing anybody into Wray, so I knew them, of course, that's why I was there. So he let them in. I think if I remember rightly, his brother had been killed or something.

Figure 26: Gerry Forrest, 2001. By permission of Robert Bassenden.

Fate had indeed hammered George and Ada Rawnsley. It had been their silver wedding on August 7, and a celebratory drink with their neighbours, the Wrights, had been interrupted by a phone call. George's brother had accidentally fallen from the roof of the church which he had served as a chorister for fifty years. They drove off early in the morning to Bradford, and when they returned their house had been wrecked.

The police report tells the official story.

A call for help had been received at Lancaster D.H.Q., and immediate arrangements were made to collect a number of men, but attempts to get through to Wray were at first unsuccessful. The A683 road was blocked at Claughton and even with the aid of heavy wagons it was finally found impassible at the Fenwick Arms. This area is a radio 'black spot', the telephones were down and other vehicles had been trapped here. It was impossible to let following traffic know. One Police car reversed until it was in a good reception area, passed on the information to Headquarters and asked that the cars be directed from the north, and meanwhile an attempt was made to get into Wray over the hills by Littledale and Winder Farm, but at one point a small bridge [Drunken Bridge near Haylot Farm] and a considerable length of road had been washed away and even the Land Rover borrowed from the local farmer was of no use.

Eventually, about two hours after the first alarm, Police reinforcements arrived at the village and set up a control point at the village Institute. Chief Superintendent Tooke and Superintendent Spence arrived and took charge. Essential services were then called to the village. Fresh drinking water was arranged by the Lune Valley Water Board who made arrangements for tankers of drinking water to be brought in. Electricity was the first service reconnected at 11.50 p.m., and the Cave Rescue Team from the West Riding ran a telephone line to Settle Police Station. It was not until 1 a.m., that it was possible by the help of the Wireless van BCJ to set up a wireless link from the Institute to the van and hence to Headquarters.[1]
(When the electricity was reconnected to part of the village at ten to midnight, Gerry Forrest was up to his waist in water in someone's cellar, and remembers a very startled moment while he wondered whether the fuse box was sharing the flood with him. Fortunately it was not.)

Figure 27: After the flood: the confluence of Hindburn and Roeburn. One back wheel of Bobbie Everett's car, the rest completely buried, can just be seen sticking out of the further sandbank. By permission of Lancashire Constabulary/ Gerry Forrest.

The media rapidly followed the police. The first in were two reporters from the *Lancaster Guardian*, and a photographer who happened to be Ruth Whittam's son-in-law:

> *To get there they travelled via Halton, the Kirkby Lonsdale road, past the Redwell Inn and through the first floodwater, then through Gressingham, where streams were raging through gardens and hedgerows had collapsed on to the road. At the Lune Bridge, Gressingham, floodwater covered over 100 yards of the road, but wasn't deep enough to stop the car engine. Hornby's main street was alive with people trying to cope with the mud and shingle left by the receding water. . . . Water was still streaming over the road through the broken wall of the castle estate beside the bridge over the Wenning, and fire engines and breakdown lorries stood by as a bus — already an hour late — led a queue of cars through the shallowest part.*[2]

The first information was out on the late night news and the national newspapers had brief but reasonably accurate paragraphs on their front pages in the morning. Several mentioned that one man was unaccounted for. This was Mr. Croft, Alice Brown's father, who was known to have been heading for Backsbottom Farm in his little car just before the flood. Luckily the car had proved unable to cope with the torrential rain and after it had stalled twice and he had seen a flood ahead of him, he had turned back and gone up to Alcocks Farm instead. A passing shiver had also been caused by the small boy who excitedly told Margaret Staveley that he had seen a dead body going down the river with its arms up '*like this*'. (The stiffened corpse of Bill Brown's unfortunate pig was discovered later somewhere towards Hornby.) The TV cameras came and went quickly, but Dora Robinson remembers four reporters sleeping on her sitting room floor. Very rapidly on the scene was the man from the North-western Gas Board. According to the police report, *He announced with some authority that there was no gas in the village and departed. His was the swiftest contribution and one of the most reassuring.*

The night was not very peaceful. At Roeburn Scar Bobbie and Patsy Everett, fearing that their house was unsafe, slept with their dogs and their pet fox in the horse box. At Stauvins Alice Brown could not sleep, but wept for the cats she had last seen running up and down the outbuilding roof before they were swept away. The *George and Dragon* was so full that beds had to be rationed — you could lie down for an hour and then make room for someone else, but no one managed to sleep. The bar was lit by the big wax candles that Mr. Burkinshaw the vicar brought over from the church, tea was constantly brewed on the bar-room fire, and the atmosphere was not entirely depressed. There was a feeling of blitz-type cameraderie. Tony Denby, who had scrambled over the bridge escorting the Rawnsleys, noted that *the Dragon was all swinging at two o'clock in the morning. I think we looked in, actually.*

The village was astir as soon as it was light. Soon after four o'clock people were out on the street to look at the extent of the damage to their own and their neighbours' houses, and the long process of rehabilitation could begin. If water lapping over Smithy Brow had marked the peak of the catastrophe, for many people on that Wednesday morning the smell from the police canteen outside the Institute, where they were frying bacon and handing out butties, was a comforting first sign that normality would return.

Notes

1. Report of P.S. 1724 Smith and Inspector Lenton of Lancashire Constabulary B Division. 23 August 1967. The official reports from this date have not survived, but fortunately copies have been preserved in private hands.
2. *Lancaster Guardian* 11 August 1967

CHAPTER NINE

Clearing up

The official organisations moved with commendable speed. The first road-blocks were set up by 7 a.m. to prevent any but essential workers and genuine inhabitants having access, although this did not stop sightseers, who flocked in their hundreds and showed considerable ingenuity in finding ways to get in on foot, and in then finding reasons why their presence was essential. One man, it is said, was very anxious for the wellbeing of a dear friend, until a local pointed out that the dear friend had been dead for five years.

Kingpin of the co-ordinated action was John Hallsworth, Clerk to the Lune Valley Rural District Council, aided by the newly appointed Public Health Inspector, Bryan Nelson, who had not been due to take up his post until the next Monday, but volunteered himself anyway.

Hallsworth's report to his Council on the events of the next three days shows a remarkable piece of teamwork in face of a situation that nobody had previously encountered. They might all have been congratulated in the words of the woman who to Gerry Forrest's amusement said seriously *It's a good job you're trained for this sort of thing.*

John Hallsworth set up his office in the Institute by nine o'clock on Wednesday morning.

Having quickly assessed the damage, and appreciated the urgent requirements, I discussed immediate action with the Senior Officers of the Police, Fire Brigade, Water Board, Electricity Board, and the County Divisional Surveyor, all of whom were already in action.... Whilst the respective services proceeded with their own tasks I concerned myself particularly with the welfare problems of the villagers and especially the homeless, including temporary re-housing, clothing and feeding. An emergency feeding centre was established in the school kitchen and was operated by the WRVS under the control of Mrs. Darlington.... So expeditiously did they get into action that a hot meal was served at lunch time to homeless persons and the numerous relief workers who were not otherwise catered for and this service was maintained until the weekend.

At 11 a.m. on the Wednesday morning I met most of the homeless in the school to obtain preliminary details of their present whereabouts and their wants, and, with the authority of the Chairman of the Council, assured

Figure 28: Newspaper headlines.

them that if necessary the Council would rehouse them all in Council Houses as and when they became available. . . . In the meantime, under the supervision of the Police, all the furniture and effects that could be salvaged from the affected houses were being taken out by voluntary helpers and placed in various buildings in the village for safe keeping, although it was apparent that a large proportion of the personal effects were damaged beyond future use. This work proceeded throughout the day, as also did the clearance of debris at the Bridge End, so that by nightfall on the Wednesday the bridge was reasonably accessible for emergency vehicles.

During the day offers of temporary housing accommodation were being received and the most urgent task from my point of view appeared to be the quick temporary re-housing of the homeless, and to assess the individual requirements, and to allocate the available accommodation in the most

practicable method I arranged to meet all the homeless on the Thursday morning.

In the meantime the Engineer and Surveyor and his workmen had cleared a channel from the storm water overflows of the sewage disposal works which would enable the sewerage from the greater portion of the village to be drained to the works and, via the overflow, direct into the river. From the Post Office eastwards the village drained towards Bridge End and, as a considerable length of sewer had been removed by the floods, no drainage facilitiies were available for that section. In addition, of course, there was no water to flush toilets. Everyone living to the east of the Post Office, therefore, was told not to use their toilets and were issued with elsan closets which had been obtained through the County Civil Defence Headquarters.

The Lune Valley Water Board had arranged for tanks to be placed at strategic points in the village to provide drinking water, and the Council's cesspool emptier was stationed in the village full of river water to enable villagers to fill buckets to flush toilets where the drainage system was still

Figure 29: Roeburn after the flood. Mallowdale Bridge having been swept away, for several months this was the only access to the Mickles' farm. By permission of Lancashire Constabulary/ Gerry Forrest.

Figure 30: Whittams', Bastows' and Hartleys' houses, later all demolished. By permission of Lancashire Constabulary/ Gerry Forrest.

operative. Both these facilities had to be kept available day and night until the weekend, by which time the Water Board had restored a piped supply to the village.

By 5.0 p.m. on the Wednesday every villager had been issued with a leaflet advising of the various facilities that were available, and generally of what was being done to relieve distress. They were also given advice as to care in washing; boiling water before drinking, and that disinfectant was available from the Institute free of charge.

At 10 a.m. on the Thursday morning, after full appraisal of the progress made, I met the heads of services and our own chief officers, in order that everyone could be kept fully informed and action co-ordinated.

By this time the main job of the Police Force was in controlling roads leading into Wray, and generally supervising activities in the village, including of course the care of private property which still remained in some of the damaged houses. The Fire Brigade performed a most valuable service in clearing houses affected by the floods; hosing out, and drying with the aid of portable drying units.

Figure 31: The Meal Bank Bridge stone, in two pieces, was found downstream towards Hornby. By permission of Robert Bassenden.

The Lune Valley Water Board had hoped to connect Wray to the Thirlmere supply through the Hornby connection during Wednesday night, but unfortunately their main, across the Wenning at Hornby, had been broken. They were installing other mains to give a supply to Wray, and had called in the Regional Water Civil Defence Officer from Manchester, who subsequently brought in the Northern Mobile Maintenance Unit which assisted in giving a supply.

The County Divisional Surveyor reported that the bridge at Bridge End would soon be repaired to permit normal traffic under control, and he was arranging for a Bailey Bridge to be erected to replace the Meal Bank Bridge, and that it was hoped that this would be completed by the weekend.

The Electricity Board were arranging to provide an alternative supply to that lost by the demolition of Meal Bank Bridge.

The Divisional Medical Officer had offered hostel accommodation to the elderly people rendered homeless, and one or two of them were availing themselves of this accommodation.

The Engineer and Surveyor reported that of the eleven houses which appeared seriously damaged, all but one were, in his opinion, dangerous and he recommended their early demolition. The one exception was a double-fronted house on the north side of the road [Miss Mashiter's] which, with special care, might be saved. In the meantime he was arranging for some of them to be propped up to prevent them from collapsing on workers nearby.

I met the whole of the homeless families at 11 a.m. on the Thursday morning and had to tell them that in all probability their houses would have to be demolished. Shortly before this meeting the Town Clerk of Lancaster had telephoned me (by this time an emergency telephone had been installed) to say that Lancaster Corporation would be most willing to help in the re-housing either permanently or temporarily of up to five families, who might be prepared to move into Lancaster, and he very kindly came out to Wray and attended the meeting with the homeless. . . . It soon became evident that all the families wished, if possible, to remain in Wray, and few were prepared to move very far from the village. . . . By this time I had had the offer of two Manchester Corporation Waterworks houses – one in Hornby and one in Caton; two or three offers of furnished private accommodation, and one or two offers of caravans.

I reached the conclusion that the most satisfactory way of meeting the wishes of the homeless was to provide caravans which could be sited in the Church Field, which the Vicar of Wray readily made available, and we subsequently accepted offers of seven caravans to house seven families for whom acceptable alternative arrangements could not be made, and these were all installed by the weekend.[1]

On Wednesday morning the village workforce had buckled to and joined the official teams. The first need was to dig out the mudfilled rooms and rescue what could be rescued. It was backbreaking work and some of it very nasty indeed. Alice Parker had just had a ton of coal delivered into her cellar and this had been in the way of the broken sewage pipe. The evil-smelling slurry all had to be bucketed out and piled in the garden.

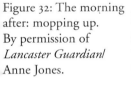

Figure 32: The morning after: mopping up. By permission of *Lancaster Guardian/* Anne Jones.

Next door, at Helen Savage's, there was only water damage. At the height of the flood, when John Wray clambered down through the gardens to help at the Johnsons' house, he remembered seeing through the back window just the lid of the Aga and a few bubbles rising. The water level fell, and a pile of test papers which Mme Bogdanoff had been

marking were still on the table, which had floated up on the water and grounded again, wet but still legible. It was not the only oddity of the kind. Gerry found a book, open and dry, also on a table which had floated. The Gledhills' car was still in its garage, but with a deeply corrugated roof, where it had been banged up and down against the roof beams.

The two top houses in the street, the Carringtons' and Swindlehursts', were saved from demolition, but had had their basements smashed in. The Swindlehursts lost not one but two pianos, iron frames and all. One of them had been recently acquired from the Institute, trundled down the garden steps with difficulty by a volunteer force, and manoeuvred in through the back door. 'That won't be coming out in a hurry!' But it did, leaving not a trace behind. Yet some of their bottles of home-made wine, still corked, were retrieved from the clinging mud. And next door, a heavy table with bulbous legs had vanished, presumably in matchwood, but there was still a mat in its usual place on the floor. The families in these two houses were allowed back to live in the street-level rooms.

They told us that we had to be very careful, and listen for sounds of cracking or anything that might indicate the building might collapse, because the foundations were badly scoured. But underneath the foundations was bedrock, and so I think we did go back fairly soon. . . . Downstairs was absolutely horrid, there were dead fish, dead animals, it was very bad. And so – the Fire Brigade came and they put great hosepipes down, and they washed and washed and washed until the mud had gone.

Across the road, the Meadowcrofts' house was almost unscathed.

We had a small porch, inside our front door, so when we went in it was a kind of a mud seal in the little porch, and when we opened the door to the living room, the carpet appeared fine, it was a red carpet as I recall with a pattern, and as soon as you walked on it there was this – squelch, and a brown sludge came up through the carpet. We were very very lucky, we probably had no more than two or three inches in our house. Now Keith Stalker, who lived next door, and whose house was exactly the same level as ours, floorwise, it was a few inches higher up the street, but that's all, they didn't have a porch, and they had probably four to five feet of water in their house. When we went back the water was spewing out of little cracks round the letterbox, due to the pressure, and we couldn't open the door, so we went through my house to the back, and tried to open the back door, and eventually had to resort to jemmying the door open because of the pressure of the water – it was quite amazing. And his furniture was floating around in there, so we just let the water out the back door in a deluge.

Figure 33: The morning after: rescuing possessions. All the right-hand houses were later demolished. By permission of Lancashire Constabulary/ Gerry Forrest.

(When the water was let out, the pretty christening dress which Brenda had bought for baby Mark in Lancaster the previous afternoon was still lying on the settee, a sludgy rag.)

Other groups were walking the Roeburn and Hindburn, looking at the damage and from time to time rescuing oddly unexpected things. It was hard to believe that the Roeburn, a sour and peaty little river in its upper reaches, had contained so many fish. They lay thick along the banks. Anthony Mickle, who was working at Bridge End Farm in Hornby at the time of the flood, remembers that people were picking up fish by the bucketful when the water subsided. (Frank Ibbetson: *I always felt sorry for Stephen Hebblethwaite. He catched a right grand fish out of the river, and Sergeant Smith saw him: 'Hey, put that back, lad, or I'll do thee for poaching'. And he had to chuck it back into the muddy water.*)

Just below the village, the bridge which carried the Little North Western Railway across the Hindburn had lost five supporting steel pillars, but while this was another illustration of the awesome power of the river, it was not a crucial piece of destruction, as the railway had fallen to Beeching's axe the year before and was disused. The fields were covered with boulders, masonry, every sort of detritus, very little of it recognizable or recoverable. But the County Council stone from the Meal Bank Bridge, though broken in two, was later found way down the Cow Pasture towards Hornby, and was set up again as a memento. Almost anything wooden had been smashed to fragments, although the Bastow's new front door was rescued intact at Pilling.

Here and there in the sea of boulders a household fridge or some other object was perched incongruously. Alice Wright's was recovered, the door tight shut, bacon and eggs still inside. It was taken back, dried out, plugged in, and purred into life. The Maughans, whose house had been swept away, recovered, a few days later, a china horse intact even to its pricked china ears, and later a green glass vase without a chip. Miss Wray's case of silver teaspoons was found at Hornby, and Gerry Forrest has in his possession a little wooden shoe.

I have it somewhere in the house because I could never find the owner. It was a Dutch clog from Arnhem that had 'Arnhem' written on the side, and it had obviously come out of somebody's display cabinet, but being wood, and being a little Dutch clog, it had sailed all the way down like a little, you know, like a little duck would do, and it had got out to Fleetwood, and they sent it back from Fleetwood.

But Bobbie Everett's Austin Westminster was identified only by one back wheel sticking out of a mud bank at the confluence of the Hindburn and Roeburn, and other vehicles had disappeared utterly. Insurance companies sometimes found it hard to understand the claims. *What do you mean, you can't find it?* one was reported as saying on the telephone. *It was only a flood, wasn't it?* Some months later, Len Richardson's vehicle was traced because its rear number plate suddenly became visible under a deep bank where the Roeburn had changed its course. *So the car's turned up – right, we'll come and collect it,* said the insurance company. *I don't think you will.*

The week ended with a real fear that Saturday and Sunday would bring an uncontrollable tide of sightseers. The bridge at Bridge End was passable again, they could not build a fortress at Butt Yeats nor control all the country lanes, and there had been good coverage in the media, which had advantages and disadvantages. John Hallsworth had the idea of passports for all bona fide villagers; these were issued by Friday evening and had to be shown at the police checkpoints on all the approach roads.

Gerry Forrest, who had not been to bed since Tuesday, had a longstanding engagement for Friday evening. He got permission to keep it, and thought with longing of getting into bed properly afterwards.

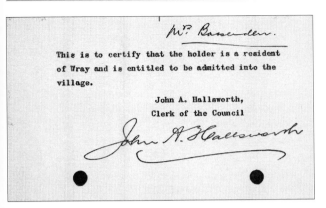

Figure 34: passports were issued to genuine villagers.
By permission of Robert Bassenden.

I'd been down to Hornby, got a bath and we'd gone for a meal out, and about two o'clock in the morning I could hear my wife arguing downstairs, at the police house, and I woke up and thought 'What's going on?' so I got out of bed and it's one of the locals saying 'I've got to show me pass to a policeman', he said. I wasn't very thrilled to say the least of it. . . . He'd had a good night out, so much so, that I said 'Now come on, get off', and he said 'Naaah — don't be like that'. I said 'I'll give you three to get off that doorstep. One, two, three. . .' 'Naay' — Pff — I threw him straight across the garden, I was livid, I was. The following day I thought 'All right, he's my first port of call' so knock, knock, and he came, he was awake, he came to the door. He said 'Eh, thou pushed me last night'. I said 'I wonder I didn't break thy bloody neck.' . . .

Notes

1. Report of John Hallsworth, Clerk to the Lunesdale Rural District Council, 11 September 1967. The official reports from this date have not survived, but fortunately copies have been preserved in private hands.

CHAPTER TEN

After the Flood

The caravan colony, at first seven, later nine families, was quickly established on the church field. Ada Rawnsley remembers that she and her husband went to Bradford on Friday August 11 for her brother-in-law's funeral, but had to be back by four o'clock to take possession of the one they had been allocated. The first rather scratch collection of vans was later replaced by better ones, which remained as homes for over a year. There was much reciprocal help in the setting up of the colony. It is remembered that the Electricity Board wanted £60 for their connection, so a village team seized its shovels and dug the trench on Sunday morning. The Bastows had a new washing machine and spin dryer which were rescued unharmed from their house, and these were established in the parish room at the back of the church. *I wash on Monday*, Mary Bastow said, *after that anybody can use them.* An enterprising dealer from Caton was soon on the scene, offering free fitting to anyone who rented radio or television from him. Water standpipes were fixed, and as autumnal weather churned up the approaches, paths were laid, and a street light appeared.

It was not ideal, and during the winter it was very cold, but memories are uncomplaining, and tend to emphasise the friendliness and team spirit. *Very very pleasant, and a beautiful view,* said Ruth Whittam.

> *We managed to survive a very hard winter in the caravan, and not being used to living in a caravan, hearing the rain falling on the roof, you wondered what was going on. But we got used to that, and we had difficulties with the stove, and we had difficulties with cooking, but we thought well, this is it, and this is what we've, you know, to contend with.*

Practical help poured in during the early days. Mr Burkinshaw the vicar had appealed on television, and a Relief Fund was set up. Although it never reached its first somewhat unrealistic target — other news soon removed Wray from the national consciousness — it raised a very useful £30,000, and, as John Hallsworth was proud to report, cost in administration only £1 from stamp duty on cheques. The speediest on the scene were the Bentham Round Table who by Wednesday 9 had handed over £15 for each homeless family's immediate needs, and with

Figure 35: The sponsored 'Wray Walk' raised £4,500. By permission *Lancaster Guardian*/Bob Smith.

other Round Tables and Rotaries produced £1000 in the first few days. A local firm donated twenty sets of aluminium cooking pans; bedding and other household goods began to come in. A Lancaster cleaning firm offered to clean and dry carpets for free, although the ingrained sludge and smell meant that this kind gesture was not very effective. The Institute became piled with enough used clothing to fit up the victims of a third-world earthquake, so that the WRVS had to organise a tactful sale at Torrisholme, and feed the proceeds into the relief fund.

Meanwhile the houses were demolished, the rocks and rubble removed, the river bed cleared and realigned, to the great delight of small boys who were allowed sometimes to ride on the heavy machinery. Much of the furniture which had been taken out of the houses was too waterlogged to be saved.

> *And most of it* [Ruth Whittam] *was just buried in a ten-foot hole down where the sewer had opened, and so they just bulldozed it into this hole and covered it up, and every time I walk over it, I think I am walking over my Welsh dresser and my three-piece suite.*

It was a matter of great satisfaction that PC Gerry Forrest was awarded the Queen's Commendation for Bravery. He also gained the William Garnett Trophy, *Presented Annually to an Officer of the Lancashire Constabulary for the most Gallant Deed of the Year,* at a time when, the county being very much larger, the Constabulary was a force of some 4500 men. The citation read in part

By the QUEEN'S Order the name of

James Gerald Forrest,

Constable, Lancashire Constabulary,

was published in the London Gazette on
14th May, 1968,
as commended for brave conduct.
I am charged to express Her Majesty's
high appreciation of the service rendered.

Harold Wilson.

Figures 36a and 36b: Gerry Forrest was awarded the William Garnett Trophy and the Queen's Commendation for Bravery. By permission of Robert Bassenden/ Gerry Forrest.

that he had showed initiative and courage at considerable risk to his own life, and that by his example and fortitude he was an inspiration to the voluntary helpers who assisted him in the rescue operation. By his leadership, organization and complete disregard for his own personal safety, he ensured that there was no loss of life in the village, and prevented an already serious situation from developing into one with disastrous consequences.

Plans for new houses in Wennington Road were being sketched by the County Architect while the damaged ones were still being demolished. Although this first response was commendably speedy, the wheels of bureaucracy then meshed. Plans for the six houses to be acquired privately and the two Council old people's bungalows were submitted in October, but the homeless families had to live in their caravans for sixteen months before they could move in to the neat, varied, and not unhandsome row. It was reported that building of the two Council bungalows began in April 1968, and by December they were 'nearly ready'. No wonder that Ada Rawnsley remembered frustration and depression as the months passed. But the architect had taken pains to give the houses more character than such housing usually gets, and thirty years later they form an attractive corner of Wray. It is only a pity that nothing tells the casual passer-by anything of their history.

Figures 37a and 37b: The bus shelter built on the flood gardens bears a high-water mark.
By permission of Robert Bassenden.

In the spring of 1968 the Bentham Round Table, which had been so generous in the immediate aftermath of the flood, organised a sponsored walk to boost the Relief Fund. May 26 was a very wet Sunday, which considerably cut down the number of walkers round the 21-mile route, but nearly a thousand took part, in the best of good spirits. Most got all the way round, Gerry Forrest and Tony Denby leading in the village contingent, and £4500 was raised. When the fund was finally wound up, it helped considerably to bridge the gaps in the private provision of the house-builders, who had by no means all been adequately insured, although the Relief Fund Committee did a good job of twisting the arms of insurance companies.

On Saturday October 5, 1968, although not yet finished the new houses were blessed at an interdenominational service of thanksgiving held on the Church Field. A wooden cross made from the timber of a wrecked house was a focus point for the 650 people who attended, as representatives of the homeless families spoke the thanksgivings – Ruth

Figure 38: Bridge End, Wray. By permission of Robert Bassenden.

Whittam for deliverance, Ada Rawnsley for the grace to carry on, Chris Wright for the help of many people, Alice Brown for the work of local government officials, Mary Bastow for the work of the services and voluntary organisations, Ann Beckwith for the designers and builders of the new houses, Ida Holme for the help of fellow villagers, Hubert Batty of Farleton on behalf of sufferers in other parishes. The Bishop of Lancaster preached, and blessed the houses. People who were there found the service both moving and satisfying, closing off the past and representing a very definite step into the future.

After thirty minutes of destruction, fourteen months of rehabilitation, Wray could feel that it was back to where it had been on August 7, 1967. Not quite where it had been. No community can share an experience like that and emerge unchanged, even though nobody can measure exactly where and in what the change consists.

CHAPTER ELEVEN

Millennium Mosaic

A village committee was set up in the winter of 1998, which behaved very properly and democratically. It started by offering a seat to every village organization, and one or two extra to accommodate the unenfranchised. Meetings and enthusiastic discussion followed, resulting in a list of ten possible projects, ranging from the statue of a scarecrow to buying a piece of rainforest for long term preservation, or putting up street lighting along the village walk known as 'the Spout'. Gradually opinion focussed on the provision of a commemorative mosaic, partly at least because Maggy Howarth, whose cobblestone mosaics are nationally known, lives and works in Wennington, two miles from Wray.

Various sites were canvassed. and various subjects, but it did not take very long to decide that the 'Flood Garden', the site of the demolished houses on the river side of the street, was the best place for such a mosaic, and if that were the site then the flood itself was the best subject. Money was available: Lancaster City Council's 'Million for the Millennium' Fund promised £5000, the European Regional Development Fund another £5000. Various other funds for rural initiatives and the village itself, notably through the Institute Committee, added more. A private donation of £500 was gratefully received. The Committee held coffee mornings. Maggy Howarth provided a design without charge, which was displayed in the Institute for the village to consider and comment on.

It was not a cheap choice. The steeply sloping Flood Garden, with its need for excavation, drainage, and retaining walls, was an appropriate but expensive site. The first plan had to be reduced, an estimate of £20,000 whittled down to £14,000. The representation was of the wind and storm spewing out a great tide of water. Some of the materials came from the Cobblestone Designs workshop – a significant part of their work is the identification of suitable beds of pebbles in riverbeds, seashores, quarries, and the getting permission to gather and bring them home. The Wray mosaic uses mainly black pebbles from a Cumbrian seashore, white pebbles from Wales, and carved insets made from green Elterwater slate. But the brown stones representing the main flood water were gathered by a village working party, appropriately enough from the bed of the Roeburn and Hindburn.

The stone-gathering was followed by a cobblestone workshop in the

Institute, where volunteers were instructed in the choosing and setting of right-shaped stones. Then at an open day at Cobblestone Designs people could see the professional set-pieces made by Maggy Howarth herself and her three assistants. Enthusiasm ran very high, and the mosaic was set up over a weekend by changing bands of volunteers, most of whom, especially the schoolchildren, will never forget the precise position of their contribution. The construction work of semicircular walls and paving was done by Richard Harrison and the Kenyon brothers, local builders, who thirty years earlier had built bungalows for the Whittams and the Bastows after the flood.

Figure 39: The Millennium Mosaic was a community effort. By permission of Robert Bassenden.

The official opening was on September 16, 2000, in front of a large part of the population, and to the accompaniment of music, poetry, speeches, and a serious tea. The infant class from the school, armed with spades and buckets, solemnly planted a crab apple tree. At the other end of the age range, the tape was cut by four of Wray's oldest inhabitants, two of whom, Ruth Whittam and Ada Rawnsley, had lost their houses in 1967. It was generally felt to be a very suitable rounding off of the story of Wray Flood.

Bibliography

Printed Secondary Sources

Booth, R F, 'Looking Back on 1967', in Royal Meteorological Society, *Weather*, 1968

Chippindall, W H, *Survey and Year's Accounts of the Estates of Hornby Castle* (Chetham Society, 1939)

Hulme M & Sparrow E (eds.) *Climates of the British Isles* (London 1997)

Farrer W & Brownbill, J, *The Victoria History of the County of Lancaster, Volume VIII* (Constable, 1914)

Delderfield E R, *The Lynmouth Flood Disaster* (E.R.D. Publications Ltd, 7th edition, 1974)

Primary Sources

Minutes of the Lunesdale Rural District Council August 1955, September/October 1956, Lancashire Record Office, RDLu

Quarter Sessions Petition, Lancashire Record Office, QSP 643/18

Royal Meteorological Society: *Weather Log* for May, June, July, August 1967

Lancashire River Authority, *Chief Engineer's Report*, 1967

Report of P.S. 1724 Smith and Inspector Lenton of Lancashire Constabulary B Division, 23 August, 1967

Report of John Hallsworth, Clerk to the Lunesdale District Council, 11 September 1967

Newspapers

Lancaster Guardian

Westmorland Gazette

Daily Telegraph

Daily Express

Contributors

Douglas Baker
Kathleen Bassenden
Robert Bassenden
Mary Bastow
Ann Beckwith
Martin Beckwith
Stan Beckwith
Nicolas Bogdanoff
Yvonne Bogdanoff
Alice Brown
Tony Denby
Mavis Denby
June Drury (Swindlehurst)
Patsy Everett
Gerry Forrest
William Garnett
Sybil Gledhill
John Hallsworth
David Hartnup
Pat Hayton
Colin Hilton
Jennifer Holt
Maggy Howarth
Edward Huddleston
Mary Huddleston
Thomas Huddleston
Frank Ibbetson
Margaret Ibbetson
Anne Jones (Carrington)
Alice Kenyon
David Kenyon
Dick Kenyon
Gladys Kenyon
Richard Kenyon

Stella Kenyon
Peter Maughan
Edward (Archie) Meadowcroft
Anthony Mickle
Brenda Mickle (Stalker)
Alice Parker
Deborah Perrins
Bertha Ralston (Maughan)
Ada Rawlinson
Ada Rawnsley
Dora Robinson
Harry Robinson
James (Jimmy) Robinson
John Ryle
Sheila Sedgwick
Bob Smith
Margaret Staveley
Allan Stephenson
Margaret Stephenson
Nicholas (Nick) Swindlehurst
Ruth Whittam
William (Bill) Williams
Sally Willis (Meadowcroft)
Mary Winter
Irene Woodhouse
Mary Woodhouse
John Wray
Chris Wright
Lesley Wright

Wray Bridge End

The houses and their occupiers affected by the flood are listed below, starting from Smithy Brow and going down to the bridge.

South side

1. (Roeburn View) Alfred Carrington, his daughter Anne and mother Mrs Kilgallon. Alfred arrived home from work just before the flood. Anne was at home because her grandmother had recently had a fall and was fairly immobile. The basement and back of the house were considerably damaged but the family were allowed back to live in the upper floors while the rest was repaired.

2. (Roeburn House) Jimmy and June Swindlehurst, Susan (10) and Nicky (6). Jimmy came back from work to the wrong side of the bridge at the height of the flood. The others were at home. The basement and back of the house were considerably damaged, but the family was allowed back to live in the upper floors while the rest was repaired.

3. (Christie Cottage) Nellie and Muriel Wray, sisters aged 78 and 73. At home. The house was damaged beyond repair and later demolished. They stayed with their nephew at Wray House, part of which was later made into a cottage for them.

4. (Burn Lea) L. and Ida Tovar. Retired couple. Believed to have been at home. The house was damaged beyond repair and later demolished. They moved across the road to 6 (north side), and after her husband's death Mrs Tovar had one of the two Council bungalows in the new Wennington Road development.

5. Ada Rawlinson and her niece Margaret Preston. Away on holiday. The house was damaged beyond repair and later demolished. They moved to Burton-in-Lonsdale and then to one of the new houses in the Wennington Road development.

6. (Windy Ridge) Edgar and Ada Rawnsley. Retired couple. Away for the day. The house was damaged beyond repair and later demolished. They moved into a caravan on the field until the new development in Wennington Road was ready.

7. (Inglenook) Chris and Alice Wright. Chris returned from work after the event. Alice was at home. The house was damaged beyond repair and later demolished. They moved into a caravan on the field until the new development in Wennington Road was ready.

8. Gordon and Jenny Denby. Roy and Kath (grown-up son and daughter). Jenny was certainly at home, the others not known. The house was swept away. The family moved to a house in Hornby and did not return to Wray.

9. Ted and Bertha Maughan and Peter (12). Ted was at work, Bertha at home, Peter out of the village on that day with his uncle. The house was swept away. They moved into a caravan on the field and then to a council house in Wennington.

10. Stan and Ann Beckwith and Martin (4). Ann was at home with Martin. Stan came back from work to the wrong side of the bridge at the height of the flood. The house was swept away. They moved to a caravan on the field until the new development in Wennington Road was ready.

North side

1 and 2. The first two houses opposite Smithy Brow appear to have been unaffected.

3. Keith and Brenda Stalker, John (2) and Mark (4 months). Keith was at work, Brenda and the children at home. The ground floor was damaged by water and silt. Brenda and the children moved in with her parents at the *George and Dragon* until it was habitable again.

4. Edward ('Archie') and Sally Meadowcroft. Sally was just home from work. Archie, held up by flooded roads, arrived as the flood began to recede. The small hall or vestibule filled with water and silt, but the rest of the house was undamaged. They did not have to move.

5. Ted and Alice Phillipson. Grand-daughter Michelle. Believed to have been at home. The house, set rather high, is believed to have been virtually undamaged.

6. Neil and Janet Walker and a child. No one at home. House closed and believed to have been virtually undamaged, but the family did not return. The Tovars (South side 4) moved in.

7. (Holme Farm) Donald and Alice Parker. Sheila (11) Andrew (8). Donald was at home. Alice and the children returned from Lancaster as the flood was receding. The ground floor and cellar were considerably affected by water and silt. The family stayed with relations until it was habitable again.

8. (Bridge End Cottage) Helen Savage (retired) and French guests M. and Mme Bogdanoff, Nicky (10). The ground floor was considerably affected by water and silt. Helen was lent a cottage in the village until the house was habitable again.

9. Jack and Ida Holme. Retired couple. At home. The house was considerably affected by water and silt. They moved to a cottage in Hornby and did not return.

10. Dick Woodhouse and Jenny Townley. At home, Dick confined to bed. The house was damaged beyond repair and later demolished. They moved into a caravan on the field. Jenny then got one of the two council bungalows in the new development on Wennington Road and Dick went to an old people's home.

11. (Bridge End House) Miss Isabella Mashiter and Mrs Annie Atkinson, sisters aged 85 and 80. At home. The house was considerably damaged. They stayed with relations until it was habitable again.

12 Jack and Ruth Whittam. Ruth was at home, Jack went to Hornby just before the flood The house was damaged beyond repair and later demolished. They moved into a caravan on the field until the house they built for themselves, behind the old one, was ready

13. George and Mary Bastow. Retired couple. Mrs Bastow senior aged 83 All at home. The house was damaged beyond repair and later demolished. They moved into a caravan on the field until the house they built for themselves, behind the old one, was ready.

14. Mrs Hartley and her son Peter Baker. Not at home. She was returning from Lancaster and held up at Claughton. The house was damaged beyond repair and later demolished. They did not return to Wray.

15. Fred and Annie Johnson. Retired couple. Two guests, names not known. All at home. The house was damaged beyond repair and later demolished. They moved to a cottage in Hornby and did not return.

Other houses affected

Backsbottom Farm. Bill and Alice Brown, their son Richard. The parents at home, Richard at work on the wrong side of the river. Nearly all buildings on the site were swept away, what remained later demolished. They moved to a caravan on the field until the new development in Wennington Road was ready.

Roeburn Cottage (at the old mill). Ivan and Sybil Gledhill (retired). At home. The ground floor and cellar were considerably damaged. They stayed with their relations at Wray House until the house was habitable again.

Three cottages on the south side of the Roeburn near the bridge were also flooded to about eighteen inches in the bedroom floor, but no structural damage.

What time was it?

It is not easy to be certain about either the time or the duration of the two separate but linked events which Wray experienced: the torrential rain and thunder storm, and the onset of floodwater down the Roeburn valley. No one was looking at their watches, and so much happened in so short a time that events telescoped for some people and elongated for others, with the result that evidence is contradictory.

There are two estimates from outside the village regarding the rainstorm. The Lune Valley Water Board engineer's report states:

> In the time of 75 minutes between approximately 3.45 pm. and 5.00 pm a deluge dropped. . . . of the type that might occur only once in several hundred years. In the short period 1.25" of rain fell at Morecambe, 3.2" in Roeburndale and 5" in the Dunsop valley.

The Lancashire Waterboard's Chief Engineer's report is somewhat different.

> The torrrential rainfall started aboiut 4.30 pm. at the north-west extremity involving Wray, and at about 7.0 pm. at the south-east extremity involving Barrowford. The duration of the rainstorm appears to have been between 1¼ to 1¼ hours, during which time upwards of 3" of rainfall was generally experienced. He also states The intense run-off from the River Roeburn caused extreme conditions at Wray Village between 6.30 pm. and 7.15 pm. (the peak at 6.45 pm.).

This is the only estimate which has been found of the actual time during which the flood hit Wray

If the second report is credible in its assumption that it took about two hours from the time the rainstorm hit the high country to the moment when the ensuing floodwater reached Wray, it seems that the start time given in the first report is the more likely. All evidence indicates that no rain fell in Wray village until some minutes after 5.00 pm. This time is given in several reports, some of which derive from Gerry Forrest's estimate, but other witnesses bear him out. Tony Denby is quite certain that he was dropped from the Council vehicle at 4.30, and knows that he walked home to Lower Broadwood before the rain began. As he crossed the bridge the river had not begun to rise. Mary Bastow is sure that she and her husband were working in the garden until at least five o'clock, when they were called in by old Mrs. Bastow who said it was high time for tea. Sally Meadowcroft left work in Bentham by the Angus Fire Armour bus at 4.45. She got out at the bottom of the village about 5.00, and hurried home up the street because it was going to rain at any moment.

Once the storm started, the rain fell with tremendous force, but one cannot be certain how long it would take for two inches of water to collect in the bowl which Gerry noticed outside his backdoor as he left his house for a first look round the village. By this time water was cascading into Hoskins Farm from the rising ground behind. There followed some indeterminate minutes of helping to clear the floating straw, then the drive down to Meal Bank Bridge with Margaret Staveley, and the hurried return to the other end of the village which he reached at the very height of the flood. The water was lapping Smithy Brow, and the three cottages had already been carried away. One may assume perhaps 30 minutes from that time until the rescues of the Johnsons and Dick Woodhouse were completed and Gerry noticed that the floodwaters were going down.

Depending on how long the rain had been falling before Gerry Forrest decided to have a look round, the foregoing can be squared quite easily with the estimate quoted above that the flood hit Wray about 6.30. This time is supported by three witnesses. John Wray believed that he left work in Bentham about 6.00, and as his narrative makes clear, he was about the last to get across the bridge in that direction. There are two witnesses who believe that in the opposite direction the 6.20 bus to Bentham got over the bridge safely. Allan Stephenson who lived on the main street opposite the bus stop, believes he saw it pass. Bill Williams, a boy of 14 on his way home to Bentham from seeing a James Bond film in Lancaster, believes he was on that bus and that it got across the bridge with no particular difficulty, although the river was high.

There is however a strong argument for believing that the bus they speak of was an earlier one. Pat Hayton regularly left work in Lancaster in time to catch that same bus which stopped in Hornby about 6.15 and got into Wray five minutes later. On this occasion it was not only held up by flood water at Claughton, but ahead of it in the queue were a fire engine and an ambulance, which had already been alerted about trouble in Wray. Owing to the state of the roads by this time, the bus may have been late, although Pat does not remember flooded roads until they reached Claughton, where the state of the A683 came as a complete surprise.

Other witnesses support the earlier time. Douglas Baker of Bentham remembers that he left work early because of the weather and has always believed that his was one of the last vehicles to cross Wray Bridge, about 5.30. He remembers water up to the parapet and a tree wedged against the bridge. Archie Meadowcroft, coming home from the University, reckons that he reached the Fenwick Arms at Claughton not later than 5.30, and found there were already severe traffic problems from the beck flooding through the village. He got through, but only just. Chris Wright reckons that it was about 5.30 when his mother rang him to say that water was coming into the basement.

As no official records remain of the alarm being raised, one can only weigh up the evidence of personal memories, which seem on balance to support an earlier rather than later time. It is clear that when the rain hit Wray between 5.00 and 5.15, the floodwater from the Roeburn was well on its way, the storm's onset at the head of the valley having been perhaps as early as 3.45. The river was certainly rising before any rain fell in the village, but the full force of storm and river seem to have coincided, as the noise of the thunderstorm masked the roar of the water for June Swindlehurst sitting behind drawn curtains. The evidence of those at the work of rescuing people from their houses indicates that at the very height of the flood the rain, though still falling, had slackened, and as the river went down the rain stopped and the sunset sky was golden over Morecambe Bay.

A careful consideration of all the evidence indicates that the full force of the flood lasted no more than half an hour, and that the crucial thirty minutes fell somewhere in the bracket of 5.45 to 6.45, but an absolute conclusion, as to either time or duration, is not possible.

Index

Occasional Papers from the Centre for North-West Regional Studies

The Centre for North-West Regional Studies, based at Lancaster University, brings together members of the university and the regional community. As well as its extensive publication programme of books and resource papers, it organises conferences, study days and seminars covering a wide range of subjects. For a small annual subscription 'Friends of the Centre' receive regular mailings of events and discounts on books and other activities.

For further details contact Centre for North-West Regional Studies, Fylde College, Lancaster University, Lancaster, LA1 4YF; tel: 01524 593770; fax: 01524 594725; email: christine.wilkinson@lancaster.ac.uk; Web site: www.lancs.ac.uk/users/cnwrs/

The Wray Flood of 1967, 2002, Emmeline Garnett	£10.95
A Fylde Country Practice, 2001, Steven King	£10.95
The Arts & Crafts Movement in the Lake District: A Social History, 2001, Jennie Brunton	£10.95
Irish Women in Lancashire, 2001, Sharon Lambert	£9.95
Hadrian's Wall: A Social and Cultural History, 2000, Alison Ewin	£8.50
Furness Abbey: Romance, Scholarship and Culture, 2000, C. Dade-Robertson	£11.50
Rural Industries of the Lune Valley, 2000, Michael Winstanley	£9.95
The Romans at Ribchester, 2000, B. J. N. Edwards	£8.95
The Buildings of Georgian Lancaster (revised edition), 2000, Andrew White	£6.95
A History of Linen in the North West, 1998, ed. Elizabeth Roberts	£6.95
History of Catholicism in the Furness Peninsula, 1998, Anne C. Parkinson	£6.95
Vikings in the North West – The Artifacts, 1998, B. J. N. Edwards	£6.95
Sharpe, Paley and Austin, A Lancaster Architectural Practice 1836–1952, 1998, James Price	£6.95
Victorian Terraced Housing in Lancaster, 1996, Andrew White and Mike Winstanley	£6.95
Walking Roman Roads in the Fylde and the Ribble Valley, 1996, Philip Graystone	£5.95
Romans in Lunesdale, 1995, David Shotter and Andrew White	£6.50
Roman Route Across the Northern Lake District, Brougham to Moresby, 1994, Martin Allan	£5.95
Walking Roman Roads in East Cumbria, 1994, Philip Graystone	£5.95
St Martin's College, Lancaster, 1964–89, 1993, Peter S. Gedge and Lois M. R. Louden	£5.95
From Lancaster to the Lakes: the Region in Literature, 1992, eds Keith Hanley and Alison Millbank	£5.95
Windermere in the Nineteenth Century, 1991, ed. Oliver M. Westall	£4.95
Grand Fashionable Nights: Kendal Theatre, 1989, Margaret Eddershaw	£3.95
Rural Life in South West Lancashire, 1988, Alistair Mutch	£3.95
The Diary of William Fisher of Barrow, 1986, eds William Rollinson and Brett Harrison	£2.95
Richard Marsden and the Preston Chartists, 1981, J. E. King	£2.95

Each of these titles may be ordered by post from the above address, postage and packing £1.00 per order. Please make cheques payable to 'The University of Lancaster'. Titles are also available from all good booksellers in the region.